THE ART OF CHEATING

RAYMOND A. SENIOR

Order this book online at www.trafford.com
or email orders@trafford.com

Most Trafford titles are also available at major online book retailers.

Printed in the United States of America.

ISBN: 978-1-4669-6557-7 (sc)
ISBN: 978-1-4669-6556-0 (e)

Trafford rev. 11/21/2012

 www.trafford.com

North America & international
toll-free: 1 888 232 4444 (USA & Canada)
phone: 250 383 6864 ♦ fax: 812 355 4082

CONTENTS

PREFACE

I did some research on the subject of cheating and had a discussion with a tourist from Sweden named Mr. Markiee Delli. He contended that most cheaters never know if their relationships will work out. Sometimes, it takes the love between you and your spouse to salvage what's left. Then, you realize and unearth the personality of the person with whom you are cheating with. They completely change. You discern that they are incapable of effective communication and the lies that they have told come to surface.

I also had the experience of having a discussion with a woman named, Mrs. Omotulto Dumoyo from Ghana. She had a divergent opinion of the matter compared to that of Mr. Markiee Delli. Mrs. Dumoyo stated that she doesn't encourage cheating; however, there are many times when the love and affection at home starts to wane and depreciate. You give it your all and Cupid turns his back on you. Suddenly, "that person" comes along who fulfills all of your desires; the desires that you have been awaiting are now satisfied. The trouble begins when you commit yourself to a trial relationship to the person you're cheating with. You wait and wait to see if your spouse is going to change, but your relationship with them remains static. This is the very reasons why divorces exist. You are unable to recreate the feeling and true love of when both of you first met. Love between two people and people in general should last infinity, but it doesn't.

Here's a scenario: Two people start off being friends-just friends. Then they make the mistake of kissing each other for the first time. "Oh my God!" are the words that seem to suffice what you are feeling. Their lips are soft and tender. Your body becomes numb as a result of this new sensation. Then you say, "Please stop. We are both married. I don't know what came over us". It was inexpressible desire and true emotion, strong enough to make you completely forget your vows; but not enough for you to lose respect for your commitments. Consequently, you accept the fact that both of you can no longer see each other, and you always see to it that you can contribute to the happiness of your husband or wife.

ABOUT THE AUTHOR

"Inspiration is like ice cream. There are many
different flavors, but just one flavor is sometimes
not enough to make you happy"

Over the years, I have experienced seeing people become separated because of the dysfunctional circumstanced created, because of this odious word "cheating". My firsthand account of cheating was with my "Dad", God bless his soul. He has cheated in perpetuation since I was seven years old and living with my stepmother. This beautiful woman never deserved to be cheated on. But, what do I know? I grew up thinking only men cheat. I was wrong. You see, I loved my step mom. She took good care of me, because I never knew my real mom. All that I knew was that she died when I was two and a half years old.

My step mom was the love of my life. She was of the Catholic religion and she could sing like a canary bird. My dad was so handsome that people called him Precious, a ladies' man. He didn't think there was anything wrong with seeing other women, because he was sowing his royal oats. In those days men were treated like Gods. They had the power.

One day I said to myself, when I grow up I want to be like my dad, in charge of my castle. My dad's friend also had a beautiful wife. She resembled an East Indian with long straight hair. They were our neighbors, but she never worked and he worked day and night. As a very hard working man, he gave her the best of everything. I decided when I became a man I was going to be more like my dad's friend.

Chapter 1

THE ART OF CHEATING

Over the last fifteen years, I have been researching the reason why people cheat on each other. Sometimes they are lonely even when you're married to that special person, or until death do us part. You spend most of your special time with him or her. You get lonely; you never get lonely the first 18 months of marriage. Those are called the golden months. You just can't keep your hands off each other. Then the Bronze season starts. The bronze season is when you can never do anything right. If you're accustomed to making love, four nights per week; which you used to do, it always makes her happy. There is always a problem. If you used to do it four different ways it still becomes a problem.

How do you lose this great feeling? In just 18 months, with all the special wonders, love, and affection you both share during dating and engagement. You spend approximately two years together, just can't keep your hands off each other. As you walk along the streets holding hands, together the only two people in the world was you both.

Have you ever stop to think what went wrong after the marriage? All the ugly girls and undesirable men become handsome and beautiful. The seventh and eight wonders of the worlds you and me changes. You are totally now are bonded together as one, you can't afford to get divorced. You have made that commitment to God and all your well wishers in church. You bought each other matching wedding bands. To

1

show your undying love and affection in this case if you are rich you can get a divorce, but if not you have to stay together. Then all those beautiful times we spend together starts to depreciate. Your sex marathon four times a week changes into every four months. You start to fuss over every little thing, at times you even have to make appointments for sex! You would put a tag on the refrigerator for whenever one has time. Sex has become a quickie, now you are in trouble. But you both go on sleeping on the end of the bed trying to keep this marriage going, you both leave for work not kissing each other like before you go your way and she goes her way.

Then one day at work, your affection shifts. The young man in the mailroom say good morning "Sandy" you look beautiful today Mrs. Henry. She becomes so flattered because your husband hasn't told you that since dating or on that special day that you got married. I feel so good.

Then you go home that evening and tell your husband, "Tony did I look good today?

He replies, "You look alright". You say "just alright". He says "yes, just alright.

Now you decide to take the mailroom guy flattery into concern. Damn, I am still beautiful! For weeks the mailroom guy keeps telling you how pretty you are. Then you ask him his name. "Roger" he replies. "And yours ma'am?" You reply, "Sandy. Just plain Sandy." Then he offers to take you out. But you didn't accept the first date. You tell him that you will think about it. She starts finding Roger very handsome. She starts falling for him. She never notices that Tony starts to come home late too. She got too caught up in your own love affair to notice Tony's lateness.

At this time, Tony was seeing someone too, but he still treats you so good. Financial, hard working pays all the bills, although it was so every three months when it happens it was still great sex. The following week, she had a Friday evening date with Roger. She came home, told Tony the same old story that she was going to the movies with the girls.

Tony got so caught up in his own affair, he never ever asked "what girls" for over a year. She never mentioned about the girls, and suddenly during that week she called him at work and asked him should she prepare dinner and what he wanted for dinner. Poor Tony start thinking that things are changing. He even had sex that week, something that he hasn't had in two months. Extra kisses, and" how's your day honey?" That week Tony was on cloud nine. But, calling his friend on the side, to keep the field level, what you don't know ever hurts. Both were starting relationships on the side.

So, on Friday, she went out with Roger, had a great time, came home later than her husband. Tony also went out to see his date. Her name was Kaisha. Like he always did after work, so there was no problem there. He never stayed over her house. He was always home by the latest 10:30pm. Out with the boys, never drinks alcohol, but always smell like a drunk. You see the reason why he smells this way is always has a bottle in his car. So before he gets home, he would take a sip and wash his face with the rum so he smelled when he got home to Sandy. She would say, get away from me with your drunken self. Sandy came in from her date at 3:30pm that night. He pretended he was sleeping but she woke him up. She told him that after the movies she went with her friends for a few drinks.

With a low voice, she says, "I want you. Now . . . damn it, right now!" So they made love. Before he could finish, she fell asleep. He was a little surprised because this never happened before. They always have great sex. But he didn't let this bother him because it hadn't happened before. She hadn't wanted to blow his cover because he was seeing Kashia.

Then Sandy and Roger became an item. They started seeing each other on the regular, almost every weekend. She is out with the girls, coming in late, really late, still Tony say nothing to her. Although he suspect she is seeing someone. He refuses to blow his cover and it was really good for him. He was getting more love from her. She didn't want him to suspect she didn't want him to suspect. One week Sandy's car broke down and Tony had to drop her off at her office and pick her up in the evening after work. Tony drove this fancy sports car and always kept it very clean. He worshipped his car. He doesn't even allow her to drive it. He was the type of guy who figured nobody can have his woman. Although he thought she was cheating, he wouldn't allow himself to believe it. He was handsome and spent a lot of time in the mirror. One of those guys, God's gift to women. Things started getting a little misty. Sandy's car was in the shop and the only way to work was for her husband to drive her. Roger owns a car but Tony doesn't know him, so he is not able to pick up Sandy even though they work in the same place. Being a cheater, you got to be professional because you will get caught. So to play it safe, let your husband take you to work. Roger and Sandy's relationship grows. If you work in the office you would think Roger was Sandy's husband. They are always close and together all the time.

Their favorite song was "Always and forever". Roger wasn't married but has a common law wife with two kids. So they were all cheaters. It was vacation time so Sandy and Roger took one week vacation the same time and save one week for their other half's but didn't let each other know.

They took vacation but pretended that they were still working. So every morning Tony would drop Sandy off, and Roger would be waiting for her. They had made reservation at one of the most expensive hotels. I mean a suite at the Radisson with Jacuzzi and the works! So they can spend their vacation in style, WOW!

The following week their holiday starts. Monday bright and early pretty boy Tony drives up in his fancy clean car. He dropped off his prized beauty wife Sandy, and passionately kisses her in front of the office so everyone can see.

Don't get me wrong, she was beautiful. They looked good together. You could say that they were made for each other (No shit). She walked into her office and he would drive off. Then straight in Roger's car they would go to the Radisson hotel by the beach. Before vacation, she told him that she was going to have a busy week. If you call and don't get me, leave a message with Shelly (her friend). Every evening, she would get to the office before 5pm so she would call him to tell him not to pick her up because she was hanging out with her friend or he wouldn't pick her up. One evening, he got there early unannounced. Waiting outside cleaning his car Roger was just dropping Sandy off from the beach. They saw Tony' car and drove through the back way. She walked in the office, opened the window and waved to him while he was cleaning his car. She shouted honey I love you. He replied I love you too honey. (Note, these are two professional cheaters). She cleaned her teeth, sprayed the same fragrance on, came out and kissed him passionately and drove off happily together.

This went on all week of the vacation. During that time, Roger would call home and ask his wife if she wanted to go to dinner with the kids. They both covered their tracks so well!

One day, Sandy told her friends that Tony will never do what I do because he is not crazy. She told them "I am the best thing that has ever happened to him.

Which man you know would wait for you to make love to him every four months and not leave? He really loves me Shelly. You know if you did that your man he would already walk out on you. Remember you have to go home and cook. I don't, only sometimes when I feel guilty. This man is my husband and we cut cake together, we have that bond and remember always make sure your man love you more than you do. He will never leave. Also make sure that the sex is good. If it fails, you are in deep shit. And Roger taught me a lot. He is so different. I just love Roger, he is so affectionate.

Chapter 2

THE BIG SURPRISE

L ittle did Sandy know that her husband who she thought overwhelmingly loved her was also playing her game. He is also seeing this beautiful girl for so long from before they even got married. To be honest, she is Sandy's friend, a bridesmaid in her wedding party. Her name is Kashia and she is much more beautiful than Sandy. She is so beautiful and sexy; she will take your breath away. She is one the girlfriend's that Sandy hangs out with when she is not with Roger. As she called him before Sandy and Tony got married. Kash and he pick out the apartment; she made the decision to take it even before he showed the apartment to Sandy. Tony and Kash made love on the beautiful plush carpet, in the bathroom, and on the kitchen counter. In other words, they blessed the place all over. John called that day. Sex on earth but I was in heaven. Kash is an intelligent girl just like Sandy. But there's something special about her, almost impossible to explain. I love those two women.

You see Tony was actually living with Kash. He sees her every day after work. He takes her to various places. He doesn't stay out late like Sandy. Every day after he leaves work when Sandy was hanging out, he would pick up beautiful Kash and take her home. She was so excited, she would make dinner in the nude and they would make love all over the apartment listening to Phyllis Hyman. Then, she would give him a bath; she would fill the tub with water and it would overflow with

7

endless suds. (Cheating is wonderful!) You see, there is nothing wrong in loving two women. Some people call it cheating, but they called it sharing. If people would only learn to share like these couples do, what a great world this would be! Isn't sharing beautiful?! Love is a sickness that doctors cannot cure. Let no one tell you that you can only love one person. Whatever and whoever your affection chooses you can love?

You see, Kash and Tony met in a very strange place—the bowling alley. Tony and Sandy used to bowl in a league for their company. A friend of Sandy invited Kash. She was absent the first night. She came by with her son. She fell for Tony. In her words . . . he had a cute ass.

After about four weeks, she decided to check out the merchandise. So she went over to him and introduced herself and said "can I buy you a drink"? After bowling, Tony replied "sure you can". So after, they went to the bar. She ordered a bottle of Remi Martin Cognac which costs around $45.00. They sat at the bar drinking and getting to know each other. During this time her son was bowling. With Sandy being home, they were not hurrying home. After drinks, Kash asked John to stop by her place so they could finish the bottle. John accepted her offer.

Kashia had this beautiful apartment in the Bronx overlooking the Hudson River. You can watch the yachts and boats cruise all over the river across to New Jersey. That night, she sent her son off to bed. It was about 11:30pm. They went back to drinking that Remi straight up, listening to songs by Phyllis Hyman. That's a voice that stay tuned in your head. Her songs kept playing as their lips came and stayed together. She told him that it was one of the most romantic nights for her. She even lit a joint, but Tony doesn't smoke. John left her house that morning at about 5:30pm. On his way home, he started to worry about what he would tell Sandy.

He opened the door, still smelling of cognac. He didn't have to wash his face with alcohol. As he went in, he checked the bedroom to see if Sandy was sleeping but she wasn't there. She was out having a good time with her girlfriends (meaning Roger). After realizing that she was out too, he went to bed but couldn't sleep. He kept waiting for her to come home.

She didn't get in until an hour after he did. She came in and turned on the bright light. "Honey, I'm home. Look what I bought you", Sandy said. When he opened his eyes, she was nude and ready. This is what she always did when she spent time with Roger to cover her tracks. She knew that he would never tell her "no".

Kashia was ready to take part in the project cheating. Two can play that game. Will they ever get caught?

The next day, Kash called Tony to find out if he was free later so he can come by. This was love at first sight. So about 5pm, Tony tells Sandy he was going partying with his boys and she knew that when he hangs out with the boys he will be home the following day. But she didn't mind because she knew all of his friends including Kashia. So off he went to meet his gorgeous and beautiful Kash.

This was his second time meeting Kash. He rang the bell and went up to the apartment. She was surprised. He said hi and asked for her son. She told him that he was out spending the weekend with his dad. Dinner was ready. She dressed very sexy in a belly shirt, very short shorts and had Jerry Butler playing "I am aware of love". It looked like it was going to be a beautiful afternoon after all. I thought we were going out to eat. I was going to offer said Tony. It looks like a stay at home party. There was a bottle of Moet and a bottle of Remi Martin. Jerry's next song was "Precious Love Means More to me". Tony was on cloud nine. Let the party begin!

He decided to call home to see what Sandy was doing but she had already left. She didn't tell him that she had a date too. But that the understanding they have between each other. They trusted each other because they had a great sex life and for people who cheat sex at home was always horrible.

So they had dinner, drank a couple glasses of Moet, and then started to drink the Moet while still listening to Phyllis Hyman. It was a beautiful evening. In fact, he spends the night. He didn't get home until 5:30 in the morning again. His wife was in bed because she had just gotten home herself. He changes into his pajamas, check his hair for sparkles so when he entered his bedroom he would not be glittering. To his surprise his wife was awake. She smelled good too. He had to make love to her as always. A tradition, when each one goes out and comes in.

The relationship with Sandy and Tony was become stronger even though they were both seeing other people. So does the relationship with Kashia and Roger and Sandy. You would not believe that Tony wasn't living at Kashia's house but even the doorman called him Mr. Tony. He sees him everyday, pick up his clothes whenever the laundry van drops it off. These clothes are his going out clothes. One evening his wife Sandy asks him to meet her and her friends at this club after work at around 8:30pm. She already told Roger that she was going to hang out with her girlfriends so as not to make things too complicated. Roger agreed that they both should take spouses out and pretend as they were doing that they are just co-workers, etc.

Now Kashia will also be there, remember she is Sandy's friend as well. So the big day has come and they both went to work, reminding each other of the time they are going to meet. That evening Tony left work and went to visit Kash, not remembering he was meeting his wife and friends. He had a drink, took a shower and changed his shirt. They all met up at the Primrose Club, their favorite stop.

Everyone was laughing and having fun, talking and meeting each other. Sandy met Roger's girlfriend, hugged her and asked about the kids. She even asked if everything was ok between her and Roger. She also told Roger's girlfriend how they talk at work and how special she was to him and how much he loves her. She was being a hypocrite and a bitch.

Then the lovely Kashia always beautiful, miss bridesmaid at Sandy's wedding greets Sandy "hi girlfriend, you look marvelous tonight". "So do you princess Kash" Sandy said jokingly. Well, Kash came first and left Tony home. He didn't get there until about 9pm. As he entered the door, everyone greets him by asking him "how is married life"? You look great. His friend's applause, Sandy didn't see him right away, she was busy frolicking with the other guests.

Then about five minutes later she sees him and noticed right away that he had on a different shirt than the one he left the house in. "Hi honey, how was work today" she asked him. "Kind of busy" was his reply. Sandy then said "was this the shirt you left the house in this morning? What happened to your purple shirt"? "Damn", he thought. He realized that he had messed up by changing his shirt at Kashia's house.

He made up a quick excuse telling her that he and a messenger had a tussle and his shirt was torn in the altercation. They were just playing. Kashia saw what happened and went over to Sandy and told her about the tussle at work with Tony. Kashia just you men play like boys sometimes smiling at Sandy walked away to see how Roger was doing. Kashia then called Tony stupid for changing his shirt knowing that he was going to meet his wife later on. He told her that he wasn't conscious of it. They both started laughing and dancing. At midnight, it was time for slow jams. All the couples danced together for a while, and then Sandy suggested that they all switched partners.

Chapter 3

CLOSE TOGETHER

The thing with these couples start getting so close that they were getting like married people with the wrong spouses. What had been happening was that Sandy and Roger was spending so much time together that she was calling her husband Tony on the phone Roger. One day at work she was planning to see Roger that evening, so she called him to have a drink but dialed Tony's number. He picked up and she said "hi baby". Tony replied "hi hon. when she heard the voice and realized that it was not Roger she said quickly "I just called to say I love you. Tony replied "I love you too honey".

After Tony hung up, he said to himself "hmmm, that was strange. She has not called out of the blue like that in a long time. What's happening? She possible really really loves me knocking his chest being proud. Then Tony called Kashia telling her he was at his desk and he didn't know what has come over him but he can't stop thinking about her, and how much she means to him. Did you know that you are my flower he said? My day and night, my everything. He was quoting love songs, love you infinity, honey me too, infinity plus she replied.

Sandy finally called the right person and told Roger her life was nothing without him. She loves him this way, meaning with his girlfriend means she will never get tired of him. You see Sandy and Tony didn't realize that practice becomes perfect. They are both cheating on each other not knowing what's in store for their relationship. Not knowing that there will be a time when they have to make a decision where the marriage will go. There is going to be a problem when their outside relationship going to change.

On a Sunday morning while they were having breakfast, Tony and Sandy decided to discuss their marriage. They have been married for two years, no children, no cats or dogs. There discussion begins. Tony says "you first Sandy". They both had an itinerary. So Tony asked, "Honey, do you want to have children? We never talk about owning a home. We are getting old. Where do we go from here? Sandy answered, I think about both ideas but what your view on it is. Tony replied "I will do anything to keep this marriage alive. So sometimes I do know what I want. It's on both of us. Sandy told him "well I'm not ready for any kids yet". "Yet" Tony asked. Are you waiting for old age or you don't love me like you used to. What are you talking about Tony? You are my husband! I really love you a lot, me too, replied Tony but I think that we should have a child. We both make good money. Angrily Sandy replied with an attitude "read my lips, I am not ready yet and that's it! Tony replied, another thing, if you find someone you love more than me would you want a divorce? Sandy replied, what were you smoking last night? Getting up asking all these questions on a Sunday morning? Of course I love you. Tony said "that's not what I asked. Answer the damn question. She replied "no one can or will ever replace you.

Sandy, I put the same question to you. Would you leave me if you find out some very beautiful girl prettier than me? Would you Tony, we made a vow for better or worst. And I will stand by my vows, but I need a son to carry on my good deeds. We will make a decision on that in the future. Like six months ok. They kiss, embrace and went back in the room to make love and prove their affection for each other. About an hour later, Sandy asked Tony to get the paper at the store. She needed him out of the house so she could call Roger. And he needed a payphone to call Kashia, so that worked out well for both of them.

This was just the beginning of what started to happen to these four cheaters. It was easy on Kashia because she was only seeing one person—Tony, but for Sandy and Roger it was more complicated.

Although Roger was not married, he had a girlfriend and two kids. His love Sandy didn't like kids so the problem begins. Tony took Kash out to dinner two nights in a row. She seemed very happy, until one night he was taking her home and asked her "have you ever read Ebony". He replied everyone reads it. It's the only interesting black magazine. She asked him "have you ever read the part that says for the brothers only. He said "yes, but it's only one persons opinion and it's the media. They will write anything to sell their magazine.

She replied "there are a lot of facts in those magazines. For instance, last week in the for "sisters only" article, she wrote about married men who are dating outside of their marriage. The article also said that most married men will never leave their wives for their girlfriend. That,' there is no future in loving a married man". I disagree after reading the article but when I lay in bed I think about us. And I think it's so true. We have been together three years before you were even married. Your wife is my co-worker plus best friend. I was her bridesmaid when she married you. If seeing their future with us just sex and dinner, let's be honest. Kash says at this point; have you ever think of divorcing her to marry me?

You claim you love me infinity, or is it I am just a good fuck, honey, be honest. Tell me, I can handle it. His reply . . . . Kash you know I care a damn lot for you; I love you even more than Sandy. Kashia reply you still haven't answered my question. Sleep on it and give me the answer tomorrow. See you later lover boy.

He left his car wondering what has come over her. Worried, that she is seeing someone else. You married guys who date outside their marriage are more jealous of their girlfriend than their wives.

So, pretty boy went home with a sad face. Sandy was on the phone with her mom. A little kiss hi honey. She replies I'm talking to mom honey. You look tired tonight. And I smell as sweet for you, your favorite perfume. She said goodbye to her mother telling her mom that her honey didn't look too well. Then she says," tell your wife about your hard day after dinner I will put a smile on your face laughing and smiling.

But homeboy didn't eat as he had a late lunch and wasn't hungry. She kissed him and told him to tell mommy what happened. Those slave drivers make my honey sad? If only she knew.

Let's talk about it. He smiles ok honey. I will take a shower so you can put that smile on my face Sandy. That's my honey; I'll be waiting for you. So in the showered, he took about half an hour singing a lot of sad songs. His last song while drying off (Me and Mrs. Jones we got a thing going on, we both know that it's wrong, but it's much too strong to let it go now, we got to be extra careful) . . . . Then Sandy opened the door and said "tell Mrs. Jones to leave you alone because I will bust her ass this you dick I mine. I ain't sharing with nobody, it's all mine, and all mine. OK! She have some damn nerves talking about kicking someone ass, while she is doing the same thing.

It seems like Tony didn't hear a word his wife said. He was depressed. Anyway he made love to her. It was the best love making that she ever had. You see he had to put out his best to cover his tracks. She said "damn baby that was good. You know you haven't given it to me this good since our first date. Ummmm ummmm honey you were great! She kissed him all over jokingly she said "you can come home sad more regularly and sing about Mrs. Jones. You really reversed it. You put a smile on my face.

Chapter 4

THE AFTERMATH

It seems like Kashia starts an affair!

Anyway about a week of thinking, she decides to just mention it nothing serious just a thought to get Tony' honest opinion. So one evening after work she called Tony and asked him to come over, she wants his opinion on something but he has to be really honest. So that evening, Tony went over and gets his regular kiss on the cheek. She made him a cup of soup which was his regular and then went into the living room to relax. Kash took a shower, came out sexy as usual, then says honey if I should find someone to make me happy like you do, you wouldn't mind I was thinking the other night after you left. You see sometimes when you leave I get so lonely, I am not seeing anyone as you know. But things come over you. Tony replied "well honey, to be honest, I never even thought of that. I figured that we would always be together. You are a beautiful woman, a friend of my wife, and sometimes I wonder where will our great relationship go? No other woman ever made me this happy in all my life not even Sandy. You are a very special kind of woman. As I have said before you are one of the chosen few; and I love you very, very much. I would really hate to lose you. (Note) what Tony was doing was refraining from answering the question. In other words, beating around the bush, Kash realized and said "please answer the question. I am not leaving yet, I just asked a question. Please honey, be honest. Answer, we are in this together.

So answer, he isn't here yet. Then Tony paused, what was the question again Kash, She became angry and lashed out at him. "Don't be stupid answer the damn question.

Then he said, honey if you should leave me, it would tear me apart. You see there is only one you and I love you. She replied "I love you too, but I need a future too. Would you leave Sandy for me to prove how much you love me? I am not telling you, I'm just asking. Tony was stumped. He couldn't answer the question.

Kash replied "you think I should live my life being a lousy second, don't get me wrong I love you. You have a week to think about it. Just remember, I am seeing no one. I'm not asking you to leave your wife; I'm just trying to see where I stand for the rest of my life. It was about 10:30pm the regular time he always leaves to go home. She hugged him, and gave him a kiss, and then he left. Poor boy was in trouble again getting home and once again feeling depressed.

Well Sandy was home, and she even cooked. After how good everything was that weekend. She looked good and smelled great. He sighed and told her he had a tough day at the office. The brewers account is messed up, really messed up. Sandy replied "I told you before never take your work problems home. Home is where we love each other. We only work on each other, she said with a smile. He said "come here honey, I love you. They had dinner, dessert and then watched the Knicks game. They played around and then off to bed they go.

The next morning while he made breakfast, he said sarcastically "you think you could find somebody you love the way you love me. She replied "to be honest, I never even thought about it. You see I am happy with what I have and that never crossed her mind. She asked him "have you"? "It never crossed my mind just curious. I was reading the Jet magazine yesterday and that's why I asked. She replied, never listen to other people's problems. Sometimes it creates problems of your own. Trust me if that crossed my mind I will let you know. She kissed him and then told him with a smile "I love you". Then they both went to work.

Those two cheaters, she was worried that she slipped up and he found out about Roger. After saying that he was reading Jet magazine, she rejoiced and said "Praise the Lord"!

Anyway Tony have a whole week to think about what Kash say to him although they still see each other every day and make love to Kash never repeat what she says to him, her deadline was that Saturday night, she was very businesslike with her love affair, that's why she stayed with him this long. She only loved one man. That Friday night before Tony was supposed to give his answer, they all decided to go clubbing. Sandy called up Kashia and told her that she and Roger heard about this new club and wanted the whole crew to go. Sandy didn't tell Tony at first, so that Thursday evening when Tony went to visit Kash she told him that Sandy was inviting the team to a new club. He told her "no problem but that he would be there after midnight. He and the boys were going to a Knicks game since they had free tickets. No problem, she told him. "I will meet you there". It was a very quiet evening, because tomorrow night Tony would have to give Kashia an answer.

Tony left his regular time 10:30pm went home to very sexy Sandy, she meets him at the door with a big kiss, guess what honey we hanging out tomorrow night I invited the crew Kash and my friend Roger will be there too. She was very happy, put him to relax on the couch took off his shirt and started massaging his whole body. Before he knew it she was making love to him, she was shouting honey you are the best he replied I know honey. That's why you married me, right honey, right, yes honey, you are the best. He said the same thing to Kash and she said the same thing to Roger. Words are so interchangeable especially the words love, sex with emotions. Then he said "I will meet you guys at the club after the Knicks game. We are going to have a great time. I haven't seen your friends in a long time; he asks do you still talk to Kashia. Sandy replies "Kaisha is always there for me. She is one of my longest friends, no one can come between us, and she is my girl.

Note—the Party

Sandy went to the office then went to Kash's cubicle to show off her leather outfit not knowing Kash was wearing the same outfit but in a different color. Two beautiful women, who were great friends but, seeing the same guy. Sandy, honey we are going to rock this party girl, work was over. Roger came down to tell Sandy see you guys later. Kash knows Roger because they work with the same company, but she didn't know that Roger was dating Sandy. Everyone was in a party mood, party hearty crew. They all arrived at the club called Garden of Eden. Sandy and her girls laughed out Great name, Eden. Girl aren't we all virgins, yeah her friends were hollering meaning Eden was the place where Adam was until God begot Eve for his companion and Eve was a virgin.

They entered say about four thirty to catch the Happy hour two dollar drinks. There was five girls in the party all the guys will be late. Roger has to pick up his girlfriend and kids at his grandmother's house then take them home before he could go out. Tony was going to the Knick game, so the girls were free until then. There were a lot of single guys from large investment companies, handsome ones. Sandy was the first to say "Girl, I see why God created men; in this garden he made some handsome and sexy ones. This is really Eden for true.

So the girls continued drinking and having girl talk. The guys kept mousing around, one started to talk to Sandy. He introduced himself as Eric. I'm Sandy but I am married if you don't mind, my husband will be here later. If you don't mind, that's ok he replied, tell him to hold tight, because you are marvelously beautiful. Thank you she replied. Suddenly Kash came over to Sandy whispering to her that shorty over there is making eyes at her. Sandy replied to go for it he might be the mister right that you are looking for. Go for it child with your fine self. Note—not knowing that Kash has been sharing her husband for a year. What a fool!

So Shorty came over neatly dressed, calm voice, about five feet nine inches, one hundred and eighty pounds. He smelled great but was missing a few teeth in the bottom but was handsome. Introduce himself to Kashia, "Hi, I'm Uriel Hutch; I just couldn't stop noticing you from across the way. You are so beautiful. I just wanna say when the father created ladies he covered all boundaries with you". She replied "I've heard those lines before but not like that. So what makes you so special, he replied I'm just an ordinary guy. I'm a vacuum cleaner salesman. I am not like those investment bankers over there. I might not be what you are looking for but that's ok. He offered her a drink, and she accepted. He gave her his card and told her "if you find time give me a call". As he walked off, Sandy ran up to Kash and said "he is so cute, you two looked good together, which bank does he work for, Merril Lynch or Morgan Stanley, Kash". Reply he is with no bank, he sells Kirby vacuum cleaners. Sandy replied "vacuum cleaner salesman, honey you can do better than that. Kash you are right, I can do better than that. (But deep in Kash's heart there was something special about that vacuum cleaner salesman and what he was doing here with investment bankers, God must have sent him, it's a sign.

It was about 9:30PM, everyone in the group was getting kind of nice so the girls went out dancing together. A few boys joined in but Uriel stayed at the bar drinking his vodka and orange juice (screwdriver). But he never participated and after about 20 minutes he was missing. She didn't even notice, and then she said to Sandy, he is gone. She replied "who Kash? Uriel. Who? The vacuum guy, Sandy girl you must be drunk. There are a lot of bankers here and you talking about a vacuum cleaner man. You're crazy girl, let's go mingle a little, you might get lucky ok.

Suddenly guess who came in, Mr. Roger. Sandy there he is, there he is Kashia there who is Kashia. Roger, she replied. Girl control yourself, you see Roger from the mailroom all the time. What's so special about him? Not knowing that they have been seeing each other for three years. Sandy was uncontrollable. Isn't he cute? Kash, girl you are drunk your husband will soon be here, forget Roger. (Note—meaning our man will be here soon, if Sandy only knew).

The other girls hooked up with a few guys while Sandy and Kash stayed together at the bar drinking. Sandy was paying most of her attention to Roger but rapping sometimes with Kash. Kash was still a little bit thinking about the man who walked into her like the vacuum man and walked out. Then, came "Mr. Wonderful" Tony with his friends. Sandy runs out of Roger's arms and into her husband's arms.

Tony came in to kiss Kash on the cheeks, and then tongue kissed his wife. He introduced his friends to the girls and everyone was having fun. Kash was a little quiet. Sandy was having a great time; her two lovers were there, although Tony had two lovers too but kinda quiet too. They all danced together exchanging partners. About 3:30am they all decided to leave.

Sandy and Tony dropped off Kash. Roger gave the girls hugs and kisses on the cheek and drove off. Then Tony dropped off Kash and watched her go into her house. They both said goodbye to her. Kash went to bed thinking about the one that got away. She looked at the card and was about to call, but controlled herself, knowing that she was going to meet with Tony tomorrow to discuss their situation.

Chapter 5

The Meeting With Tony Then Life Changes

S o here comes the Saturday meeting with Tony where the whole live affair between Kash and Tony either gonna last forever or going to an end. That morning before Tony left home he says to his loving wife Sandy "honey I'll be home late tonight because we at the office still haven't solved the problem with the Brewer account and I don't want to bring my office problems home. She told him "no problem". I will see if Kash want to go to the movies with me later. Tony already knew Kash wont' be able to go to the movies with her, they both kiss each other goodbye. As Tony got to his car he called Kash to tell her Sandy was planning for them to go to the movies. Deep inside Tony didn't realize Kash was Sandy's excuse to meet with her friend Roger. As Sandy reached her office she went to Kash's cubicle to invite her to the movies. Kash said she had made plans a week before to meet with her brother and his wife and kids so Sandy hurriedly calls Tony to tell him she will go out with Ingrid and Stacy, her other friends because Kash had plans to visit her brother. It was really a tough day at work for Tony. Tony really loved Kash and if Sandy had given him an ultimatum to make that decision it would be easier to leave his wife, than lose his girlfriend. You see your girlfriend is always there to cheer you up when things go bad at home. You can't ask your wife to do that when you fight with your girlfriend.

So about 6pm Tony called Kash and asked if she needed anything, she told him to buy a bottle of Moet Champagne, you know I love Moet, the same way I love you. Tony smiles, so it's decision time. For this five year old love affair to either last longer or dissolve in plain old fashion friendship. Tony arrived with a chilled bottle of Moet which Kash put in the refrigerator and got him his favorite cup of tea, Chamomile. She turns on the stereo and put in a CD, Brenda and the Tabulation, first song, where there's a will there's a way and I'm gonna make you mine someday. Poor Tony thought the song was for him.

But from Kash's made eyes on Uriel, she never stopped thinking about him all weekend long but she didn't' want to call before she found out which way Tony's decision could go. Anyway, the next song was "For the good times" by Al Green. So Kash asked him "Did you think about this real hard over the weekend"? He said "I couldn't sleep and I tossed and turned so much Sandy sent me to the guest room".

Honey, you know I care about you. As Baby face said in that movie 'I've been loving you so long, it's really hard to stop now that's what Otis Redding said. But life is not fair and you and Sandy are best friends. It's hard to lose either one of you, I love you both forever, no matter what decision I make tonight" and then he started crying and sobbing loudly. Please honey, give me more time.

Kash replied "you can't be damn serious. I have played second fiddle with you to my best friend for five long years and you still asking for more time? I am twenty five years old, and been with you two years before you got married. Come on Tony wake up you still sleeping. There is nothing in this for me but heartbreak. You know you're not leaving Sandy and I am not asking you to either, she is my best friend but come on honey have a heart, if it continues this way, there will be no more juice left when I find the right person. She cried a little tear and say I am beautiful I need somebody for myself, we can still be friends, but this is it.

Then Tony you are talking like you already find Mr. Right already. She replied "when I find him you will be the first to know. You will meet him then you can tell me if he is right for me and you better be honest, or I will hit you upside your head. You know I love you, but I need what you have too, a husband. I don't want a rich man I just want someone to love me the way you do, someone to come home to, someone to cook for, and shower him with kisses. The night ended with tears hot with emotions. With the song "So in love with you", they hugged and Tony left and said to her "this is not the end, someday we will be together, I have time, I have nothing but time someday you will be mine forever. Goodnight love, see you tomorrow evening". She replied "no Tony, that's over with. From tonight, we are just friends, we talk on the phone, and we meet together with your wife, Tony please give me some time, that's the only way this is going to work. We will talk. But no coming over unless Sandy is with you, please understand. Honey I need my space, please ok Tony said his last words are I ain't got to love nobody else bye.

Another sad night going home to Sandy but tonight a big surprise Sandy was not home and it was 12:30am. He approaches and open the door, hi honey I'm home. No answer. He checked everywhere no Sandy. No feet rubbing, no fragrant smell, nobody messages, both his women deserted him, give sometime by himself to mediate.

About 1:30am Sandy came in, didn't ask any questions, it was Saturday night so 1:30am was early. She yelled "honey, are you sleeping? You better not, I had a few drinks and you are mine tonight. He said honey, I'm not in the mood, she replied "when I get out of this bathroom I will make you in the mood, she came out of the bathroom in this black negligee the one she wore on her honeymoon night. She turned on the bright light and he was instantly ready. Tony, honey you are so beautiful, she started taking him apart. She didn't even have sex with him, just pure love; she knows what turns him on. He instantly forgot about Kash for the next hour. Then he says it was a very tough day today. I needed that release, that's why you are my wife. (Not knowing that she just came from the Marriot with Roger. As the old saying goes "if you don't know you don't know.

Tony slept like a baby hugging his wife; he woke first and made breakfast, although it was Sandy's morning to make it. Sandy slept late.

He called Kash. They talked for a little and he lied and told her that he couldn't sleep thinking about the breakup. She said she tossed and turned too, but life goes on. He told her he made breakfast and asked her if she wanted him to bring some for her. She said she was going to IHOP to eat and relax.

Before she left, she made that phone call to Uriel, and asked him how his weekend was. He at first didn't recognize the voice because they hadn't talked on the phone before. So she reminded him Kashia—the lady you gave your card to on Friday night. "Oh, he replied the Indian princess. He said I see you in my dreams all weekend, so pretty so fine. I dreamt about an angel look just like you, so how was your weekend? I hope, not as bad as mine. I stayed home; I am studying for my insurance test. She replied I would like to come over one evening next week. My vacuum is not working too well. Which day would be good for you? I have an opening on Wednesday at 7:30pm is that ok. She said yes, and gave him her number.

Afternoon Sandy called to tell her she miss a great time last night she had so much fun. Telling her she was worried because she came in real last and Tony didn't say a word, that he was a great husband, one who isn't insecure, but understanding. Kash replied that's great I hope I find someone as good as Tony. Well Sandy said, there was did you call your vacuum salesman yet? She said I called him today, he sounded so sexy on the phone, he hardly talks in face he is coming over Wednesday to clean my carpet, but Kash you only have a small rug. It's dirty and needs cleaning badly, she replied. Is he going to clean both rugs? The rug downstairs haven't been cleaned a long time, sure your right girl, Kash replied. Little did she know that her husband been cleaning this rug a long with hers she smiled.

It was Sunday and Sandy invited Kash to dinner, she said no I'm going to relax today, about 3:00pm play some music. About 5:30pm Uriel called to ask her what she was doing and she told him that she was playing CD's. Please play this song and think of me. "For your Precious Love", by Jerry Butler. She replied I don't have it. Ok then, he stated "I will play it for you. Put your phone on speaker she did. After listening she replied great words. Jokingly she said you play this for all your girlfriends. Uriel if I had a girlfriend I wouldn't be home, me and my ex-girlfriend broke up about 6 months ago. She was a nice lady but a little insecure so we broke up. In fact while I am on the subject let me tell you about myself. You didn't ask. Kashia replied "well Uriel I think you wait until we meet face to face and then I will tell you about me and you are so different. One question, are you from Trinidad, I hear an accent. No, I'm from Jamaica. It is true what I heard about Jamaican men? What did you hear? That they all have a big bamboo, I don't know, he laughed all I know is mine is very very small. Very funny my Indian princess, I just want to say again you are a very beautiful woman and I mean it. I just can't believe your single. Kash it's a long story and it will be told to you, I will call you later say about 9:30pm before bed. Bye.

At about 9:27pm Kashia phone rang. "Hi, guess who? Uriel, no you wrong, Tony, Tony who? Anthony what you want Tony? She was abrupt then Uriel replied Why so rough? It's me Uriel, my middle name is Anthony it was only a joke. But doesn't know her ex-boyfriend's name was Tony. She then apologized saying she thought someone was playing games with her. I was just about to call you. Dude, yeah man Tony says in Jamaican. I man just use my eyes to cast a spell on you girl. Now you can't leave. You are fe me gal now. Uriel you are so funny, then chat a couple of hours then said goodnight.

Monday morning Kashia wakes him up asking if he had breakfast. He said he doesn't eat so early and off he went to work. Kashia went to the office all happy. She finally found a friend who wasn't involved with Sandy and not feel guilty. After about half an hour in the office, Tony called, he was calling all weekend but Kash was monitoring her calls, as usual he asked about her weekend and told her he missed her. She said, you'll get over it soon. Sandy and Kash went to lunch and they talked about Uriel, Sandy was happy that Kash was happy, so they could go on dates together. Well things start looking up for her Kashia but there was a little trouble going on with Sandy, she finally tell Kash she has been dating this guy on the side for about two and a half years, but Tony doesn't know anything about it, you are my best friend it's our little secret. No problem replied Kash, everybody does what makes them happy, sometimes you need a little flavor. Then Sandy tells her it's Roger in the mailroom. She sighed, oh you mean Roger, he seems to be a pretty nice guy. But sometimes I see him with a lady and two kids in his car, did you know he has a family. Yes, he told me, but honey she is so sweet of late he's been acting kind of strange. We have been seeing each other for a long time but we kept it a secret. I know Tony doesn't know anything about this it's just us, who to tell if Tony wasn't seeing someone too. But I hope he isn't. Kashia replies you know Tony loves you and I'm sure he will never cheat on you, when he's around you, he can't keep his hands off of you. I'm looking for a relationship like yours; I just admire how much you guys love each other. And you should stop seeing Roger. There will never be another Tony and leave Roger and his family. I only hope that things work out with Uriel and me. I really like his personality, and I am getting older. I really need love or someone in a serious way. Sandy, honey, if you love him give it a try, I'll be happy for you. So when are you going to see him again? He will be at the house Wednesday to do my carpet. I hope that we click girl. Sandy said, thanks for the advice, but I will not give up on Roger. He is so sweet, but you know Tony is number one. Chat with you later, Bye.

Chapter 6

SANDY IN TROUBLE

They Met

After Sandy gets home, Tony wasn't there so she called Roger to tell him Kashia had seen him with his family and she even said they were cute, but she didn't know we were seeing each other, so I told her, but that's no problem. She won't tell Tony, she is my best friend. Soon after Tony comes home, hi honey how was your day? Fine said Sandy, yours okay. Sandy continued to talk to Roger, she was in the bedroom, Tony was in the living and dining room getting himself something to eat and watching the news fro about an hour. Kashia ran threw his mind so he decided to say hello. He picked up the phone and overheard Sandy talking to Roger, they weren't saying anything concerning their relationship, just about his family matters, so Tony didn't get any idea. Tony entered the bedroom, who are you Dr. Ruth," Telling people how to run their lives". Sandy asked him "were you listening to my conversation, no honey I just picked up the phone and I overheard. I thought that you were off the phone, who was that anyway? She replied "one of the guys want Kash's number. I see, want some woman's advice, he having a little problem at home.

After, she finished talking to Roger; Tony picks up the phone to talk with Kash a little. Kash asked" who is the new girlfriend," now that they stopped seeing each other. He said that now he was going to take a break and see if he can get over her. Tony said "I heard about the guy you met at the club, you really like him then go for him girl. Although, I am jealous, you really need someone. Good, you are a great lady.

Soon after Tony hung up, the phone rang, it was Roger. Tony answered the phone. Roger asked for Mrs. Henry. Tony called her and told her it was her co-worker. So they continued their discussion. Roger telling Sandy his fiancée wanted to get married and he thinks that she really deserve to they've been together for nine years and if that should happen would it be ok with her. Sandy replied "I don't know, we will cross that river when we get there. Sandy was getting jealous. But she already knew Roger had a family and she was married so why show jealousy. She was afraid of losing him, Roger just wanted his family to be happy so he could continue dating Sandy. He loved both ladies and Sandy wouldn't give up Tony. Anyway they changed the conversation and Roger told her "we will see where we go from here.

So the big day soon arrived, the meeting of Uriel and Kashia. Wednesday came around too fast. Uriel called Kashia to confirm their appointment say around 6:30pm. Kash went home and cleaned up before Uriel reached. She made sure everything was clean off the rug. AT 6:30pm the doorbell rang. She let him in, and he had this big box. She couldn't believe a vacuum could be that big. He took out this shine machine named the Kirby. Oh, she cried, this is the great vacuum I heard about. He replied "this isn't just a vacuum, it's a homecare system, and it'll even cut your hair.

Anyway, Uriel started his rap telling her the history of the Kirby showing all the components that comes with it. He vacuumed the rug then shampooed and dried the rug. She kept on asking the price after he finished drying the carpet. He vacuumed the mattress, did the drapes, and showed her how she can own it. Total price down was one thousand five hundred dollars. How you would pay for this, he asked. We take credit cards, with cards we give a special discount, plus we give you five hundred dollars for your old vacuum. So give me eight hundred dollars on your visa now. She said for eight hundred dollars

I will take it, here is my visa. He asked her for a drink of water. She said, how about some juice, so he had juice. Her other friend next door called and told her that she was unable to do the movie, Kash forgot she had a date with her neighbor to go to the movies. Anyway Uriel overheard her conversation and said if she don't mind, he would do the movie with her. So they went to the movie that night. You see that night was Kashia's birthday, but Uriel didn't know. Anyway they had a great time at the movies. He dropped her off that night and they kissed goodnight, but it wasn't a little smack, it was real tongue involved. You Kash are a great kisser, replied Uriel. You too baby, replied Kash. She was so caught up in the kiss she forgot it was the vacuum salesman; it was like they had met before. Their emotions ran wild. Before Uriel left she said, "Promise me it's not just tonight, we are going to continue seeing each other. Uriel, girl your kisses are so sweet that I am never going to kiss anyone else again. See you tomorrow, and they kissed again. The minute Uriel got home, he called and they spent hours on the phone. The same night Uriel told her about himself, he was married and had two kids. His wife was abroad, they had outgrown each other because they got married so young, but he still supported his kids. They go to a private school, but he hasn't been with his wife for over eight years. Because of the circumstances it wasn't possible, but he loves his kids.

Then she tells him about Muslim College in Florida. She was married under the faith at nineteen something she haven't even told her friend or ex-boyfriend. She was married for two years, then they separated and got a divorce. She came back to NYC and lived with her parents but they were always telling her what to do, and then she found her apartment. She asked him whom he was dating before her. He said, he had a girlfriend who was very jealous and at the time she wanted to fight him, but he walked away. He doesn't believe in hitting a woman so he decided to split. All of a sudden she was pregnant, because she believed that if she had a baby it would force him to stay. He admitted the kid was his, but still don't want to see her. He will always support his kids. He told her the story about himself.

You see Kash my mother died when I was six years old and my dad left me at ten. I haven't seen my dad in twenty years. I grew up with my grandmother. It's a long story, but if we keep this relationship you will know a lot more about me. I hope that we will continue seeing each other. She replied, "I hope so too". (You could tell that these two were falling in love, from the first time they met each other at the club). And for a long time, the two love birds continued seeing each other. Kashia was much younger than Uriel. You see Kash's stepfather was much older than Kash's mother, and she had ssenn how he took care of her mother. She had married a man in her own age group but never got much affection so she decided to see how things would work out with Uriel, an older guy.

Their relationship started to blossom and she never told Sandy or Tony the details of their friendship, but they were close. Sandy was glad she found happiness so they could double date together. Kash and Uriel actually live together but had their separate apartments. He spent most of his nights at her place, and sometimes she visited his place, but he was mostly at her apartment. They spend a lot of time doing dinner and going bowling. Uriel was a soccer freak; he loved the game, and was a great player and previously owned a couple of teams. He loved the adventure of learning new games.

These two love birds went together for about six months before having sex. It was Kashia's idea. She was of the Muslim faith and Uriel respected that. Uriel was Jamaican and was accustomed to making love on the first night. Jamaicans are hot-blooded. But he waited and claimed it was good, as the saying goes, good things come to those who wait. Kash also taught Uriel how to bowl.

The vacuum cleaner business was good while it lasted. Uriel was a great salesman, and Prudential Insurance Co. was hiring so he decided to apply for the job. He went for the interview, did well and decided to try the corporate ladder and see how far it took him. He got the job and now he was working for a top five hundred company. He was very ambitious to make it in the land of opportunity. Things started looking up. He changed his car from an old beat up Chevy Nova to a beautiful Oldsmobile Cutlass supreme. He got a lot of support from Kash. Although they lived apart he bought her a used car too and his insurance license and pass them both. But there was one problem Uriel felt Kash was pretty young and in the back of his head there was this feeling that whenever she found someone she loved younger than him, she would leave. Uriel started feeling insecure after nearly two years in the relationship.

She would always go out with Sandy and friends after work. The movies, and other places. Whenever he was at work his job demanded long hours. Kash told him there was nothing to worry about if she wanted a young guy she wouldn't have dated him. Their relationship went on and on until Kash asked if he was going to divorce his wife since they have not lived together for so long. He said that he would think about it. She told him to start thinking now. Meaning, she was ready to settle down. She didn't intend to have what happened to her and Tony to happen again. So one morning Uriel called a meeting at the breakfast table to discuss the situation.

You see Uriel didn't mind divorcing his previous wife to marry Kash, but he wanted it to last a lifetime. In the back of that thick head of his, he still figured that because of his age, she would leave him later, so he came up with this idea.

The idea was they should separate a while, call it a trial split. Each person should go out and see if there was someone else they fell for and if it doesn't work out, then they would get back together. That Sunday morning they both sat at the dining table and each would write why they think they should separate to prove their love, then back together. This idea was Uriel. Kash agreed but during the separation they would still see each other frequently. Uriel said we start this at the end of the month.

Uriel started staying home a lot. In fact he went to learn to bowl properly and joined a bowling league. The apartment Kash was living in was a studio so they decided she should get a one bedroom, so she moved into a bigger place under the understanding that when they got back together they would have a bigger and better place. This place was beautiful right by the park, great scenary. She loved it! She moved, Uriel moved all his clothes back to his apartment and they went further away from each other. Now they correspond on a daily basis, but they started to grow apart a little. Kash started to correspond with her ex-husband and had already decided not to get back with Tony, her other ex-married man. Uriel was staying single and waiting for Kash to decide. They had dinner together and even made love sometimes. One night Kash called Uriel and told him she was corresponding with her ex-husband again, and what he was doing. He said he was doing the same as before talking with his wife from Jamaica. You know she have the kids, so we have to talk. Not talking to my son's mother, she out but can go out and have fun. But always remember our agreement. All I'm doing is bowling. He even invited her, Prudential had a team on his job.

After, four months of separating, Uriel had a secret admirer. But, she just said hello. She was this fine substitute bowler, very beautiful and had a ten year old son she. She was always paying special attention to Uriel. He told Kash about it and she said go for it boy that's the only way we will find out if we love each other. Uriel asked her if she and her ex-husband was still corresponding. She replied "yes. He came over on Saturday and we talked for a long time, she also told him that she was working in the insurance business and got engaged, but would rather us getting back together. I said we should think about it more and more. Uriel you know that I love you. This was all your idea. No problem, he replied, "if we were made for each other non one can separate us, no one.

Friday night was bowling night. Uriel was always early so he could practice before the game. That evening, the sub bowler and his son was early, so while Uriel was practicing she came over and pat him on the shoulder. She said "after your game I would love to talk with you". She waited until bowling was over, she said "big boy I've been watching you for a long time. I watch your ass. As it goes up and down the lane, did you know you got a great ass. Anyway can I buy you a drink? Uriel accepted, her son was playing video games so she took him to the bar and bought a forty-eight dollar bottle of Remy Martin. They drank for a while, then she introduced herself as Vohn. He introduced himself as Uriel and told her it was a pleasure to meet her. He told her she was so beautiful and said "you are the beauty of the men's eyes, why me honey. She replied "look around the alley, no man in here have your ass.

I've been asking the ladies about you, and everyone likes you, baby when I see something I like I go out and get it so no bullshit. I really like you. Even give me a chance to love, by the way if you have nothing to do later I would love for you to stop by my house. I will make sure your boyfriend is not there. I don't want to die now. That's a joke I'm just joking. I will stop by since you asked me to. Where's your son. Is he ok with it. Come on Uriel she said he is a kid. He doesn't make the decisions. So there was still a half of the Remy left in the bottle and we took it home. Well Uriel seemed to be moving up you see. He was now driving a Cutlass Supreme and she drove a Cadillac Berity top of the line. Anyway he followed her home and found a spot for his car. Then he jumped in her car to the indoor garage at this beautiful building and went upstairs to the 25th floor with a beautiful view. It was about eleven o'clock and she sent her son off to bed. She placed some tapes in the player all Phyllis Hyman. They drank the rest of the Remy Martin all night, and Started drinking some "Stones Ginger Wine". Uriel stayed until about three thirty that morning, and then he went home. Later before he left Vohn told Uriel she intended to see him about midday. She told him she was going shopping and would love his company. No problem, he told her. "I don't have anything planned so far". Uriel called up his friend to tell him about this priceless chick.

But Uriel was still in love with Kash. He made her a promise and he intended to live up to it although he suspected she was trying to get back with her ex-husband. They had become estranged; hardly saw each other but they communicated on the phone. Uriel told her about Vohn the lady who picked him up at the bowling alley. Then he said she is rich, Kaisha said to go for it but don't forget poor old me ok. I love you and we had an agreement. Uriel I will never forget you no matter what.

Vohn and Uriel became an item. They saw each other regularly, so regular that most of his friends don't see him anymore. She was very possessive and she didn't want him around anyone else but her. In face, most of Uriel's clothes were at Vohn's house and whenever he was out of clothing, she would buy him new ones. She was really in love with him and Uriel was in love with her too. According to Uriel, it was the best sex he ever had in all his life. There wasn't a woman who treated him with so much affection. She would call him at work to find out when he is going to be home, and on his way home she would set his bath while preparing his food. When he got home, she was dressed very sexy for him, and smelled great too. You could smell that fragrance as you stepped from the elevator. As he entered the door she would greet him with a kiss. Not just one day but every single day. Sometimes she would strip him naked as he entered the door, turned down the stove, and make love to him in the living room before dinner. She wasn't a nymphomanic but I suppose he gave her good loving too. Loving, that she never got elsewhere. These two people were really in love with each other. Uriel still talked with Kashia but never made love with her anymore because Vohn never left his side. They were always together. His friends claimed that he was whipped because he hardly saw them anymore and only at work. After work, Uriel headed straight home to her.

This relationship lasted for about two years. There was no time for anyone else but there was a problem. The problem was that they were both drinkers. Vohn smoked and Uriel didn't. Vohn smoked a joint every night and whenever she smoked she wanted more and more affection and more sex. Over the period of their relationship, there was doubt in Uriel's head that if she went away without him, and smoked she would cheat on him. Other than that, everything else about her was fantastic. She was a great woman.

It was coming on to Christmas time so they both planned a vacation. They wanted to go to Hawaii. Everything was finalized for the trip. They always fantasized how much fun they would have on the beach in the islands. How they would take each other apart on the beach and make love until the sun goes down every day on their vacation. Then there came a problem. Uriel couldn't go on the date and the tickets were not refundable. You see Uriel had to complete his assignment for his year end quota at his job. So he had to cancel this trip but decided that she could go and take her girlfriend with her, although their was doubts. You see when you go on an island there are a lot of players and single men waiting for single tourist to date and help them enjoy their vacation. Lots of drugs and marijuana are involved and knowing how she acted when she smoked, it created fear but the only way to get over these fears is to let her prove herself.

So the day for the big trip arrived and he took them to the airport. They couldn't get their lips apart for the goodbye kiss. It was like they were twins stuck together. Off she goes, you could see the tears falling down Uriel's eyes, he already missed her. After she left, Uriel slept at his apartment instead of hers. You see he never gave up his apartment. He called Kaisha and asked her out to the movies and went bowling with his pal. He also played softball and soccer and went back to his regular routine. She called everyday, but he could hear something in her voice. He asked her "honey do you have something to tell me. You don't sound happy". "No honey, I'm having a great time. I miss you a lot. Really I miss you". Uriel had his doubts, anyway Kaisha and her husband was still trying to get back together but he was living in Texas (Houston). She was unable to decide if it was the right thing to do so she asked Uriel his opinion. He told her "give it a couple of months. Don't rush it you might be making the wrong decision, but anything you do I will be right here for you.

One night about 10:30pm, Vohn called Uriel and said that she had something very important to tell him. Uriel was confused. "Honey, are you all right. Did you have an accident while driving? Is your friend ok? She told him everything was ok. "Then what's so serious that you have to tell me. I made a big mistake. Uriel what are you talking about. Don't tell me you made love to somebody else. Don't even try it. It's unacceptable. Then she said "honey I'm sorry, the first night I landed. We were on the beach smoking some grass and I don't know what came over me". "Tell me it only happened once". No honey it happened more than one time. I am sorry. I love you. I fucked up bad this time". Then Uriel asked "so I suppose you fell in love with him like the way you fell for me too". "no honey" she replied, "but he is a nice guy".

Uriel fell to pieces; he was very much overwhelmed and refused to see anyone else. He was broken hearted and stayed home for three weeks just listening to sad songs. He was messed up real bad. His cried his heart out. Vohn came back and he went to her apartment to pick up his clothes, and then went home. He wanted her back. There goes the best sex of his whole life. Two weeks after she came back, the guy she met in Hawaii came to the states to visit her. That made Uriel hurt real bad. She had the heart and introduced him to everyone as her new friend. They were all surprised because they all loved Uriel. He was so embarrassed he stayed away and got a phone call from her saying she was sorry and she wanted him back. Uriel decided that since was good, he would use her the same way that she used him. This was hard to do because he loved her so much.

Uriel went back and begged Kaisha to make the decision on their future but she was still trying with her husband. Kash and Uriel started seeing each other everyday. He finally gave up his apartment and moved in with Kash, but was still making love to Vohn. About six months after Vohn started to date a friend she knew a long time ago. She even got married and Uriel and Kash got engaged. Sandy was happy for her. She and Tony was at the party. Roger was also there. His wedding to his kids mother was also coming up. Sandy was angry because she was losing Roger. Sandy's birthday was close so she kept a big party at the house. There were a lot of beautiful women there as well as a few new employees from her job.

Chapter 7

AT THE PARTY

Sandy's birthday party was special as it was her thirtieth birthday. There were a lot of new faces but her favorite face was that of Roger. Knowing how long they had been together and today might be the last time that she would be seeing him. Everybody was in a party mood. Tony was very happy with his wife with whom he had spent six beautiful years with but still hadn't achieved their goal of having a child in their lives. So the party begun with Tony as the master of ceremony welcoming everyone telling them how glad he was that they were there and how happy he was to have Sandy as is wife. But there was one thing missing and he was going to work on it tonight. Everyone laughed. So Sandy said "honey, what's missing?" We have everything, each other, and we love each other very much." Tony said "we need a child and I want to start working on it after the party". (jokingly) Everyone laughed. Kash said what's taking you guys so long. I always wanted to be a godparent. Come on guys do it now. Sandy replied he is going to be swinging from the chandelier tonight if you guys fell an earthquake it's Tony and I making Junior, so lets drink to it now.

The party was great, there were a few new friends, Uriel and Kashia stayed very close together. Roger was a little quiet because he couldn't play with Sandy as he wanted to. There was something Roger wanted to tell her about him and his fiancé and his kid that they were thinking about leaving to Florida. Tony was unable to tell jokes to Kash as before because Uriel was there. Sandy already invited Roger's replacement the stock broker at the party. He was there with a few of his friends who date girls in Sandy's office.

Everything went well until about 4:30am. People started leaving. Roger said he had an announcement to make. He told everyone how he enjoyed their friendship for the last three years and special thanks to Sandy, Tony, and Kashia. He told them he got a job in Fort Lauderdale. He already found a house and he was relocating. He told them he was going to miss them but that they would get together again sometime. He jokingly said "I hope these two couples all the best as they plan their additional to their family tonight. They were both good to me. You too Kashia and Mr. Uriel don't hurt my girl (Right). It wasn't really surprising to Sandy because they talked about the splitting up before, but she was shocked to hear about the relocation. The party was over. Almost everyone left but Sandy's stockbroker boyfriend Sean and his friend stayed a while to have the last drink. Tony was packing up the presents and Sandy walked the remaining guests to the door. She hugged Sean, this was their second meeting and Sandy was also noticing Tony trying to make moves on her co-workers. After she came back, she said "Tony boy, I say you making moves on that new blonder from the office old boy. I didn't know you loved blondes" she said sarcastically. Tony replied "I was just entertaining our guests. I could say the same about you with your stockbroker buddy of yours". "Tony honey, there is no need to worry. We have been married for so long and we have been honest with each other. Cheating will be the last thing on our mind. You know there are so many marriages that broke up since we got married and we are still together. I personally never even have the reason to think anyone of us would cheat on each other because we are totally committed to laws and rules of married couples and how they operate. I want our union to be like grandma and papa who have been together for 43 years. We are in the process of starting a family which will keep us more together. Tony I have never thought that you have ever cheated on me, our romance is still great, the sex is just like when we first met, now you tell me why do couples cheat on each other? There have to be a breakdown in their home. Romance and honey I am totally happy with the way we do things. There's no insecurity in this relationship, we give ourselves the freedom to do whatever we choose because we love each other. You see honey true love is pure its' the way you love and I love you. It's unexplainable, durable, the way we kiss, the way we hug, the respect we give each other, and when you love someone you have to keep your sex life active, because if you ever slip up there's always someone to replace you. So honey I am glad you are always here for me and trust me nobody will ever be able to replace you, never, never!! (Sandy). Honey I am so moved by the things you say, I totally believe in honesty. I feel true love should last forever and what we have is irreplaceable. We have found true love from our very first date, and here we are four years later talking like we just met. I love you Tony baby, always and forever. They hugged and kissed and then off they went to Loveland. They went on to make Tony junior or Sandy junior.

Note: These two people are in love, married and have been cheating before they were married. Although they continued their cheating they never disrespected each other. Each are clueless of the other's relationship with others. Because they continue making love better everyway to each other, so there's no reason to suspect cheating, because of what they learned outside. If it's good they discuss it in the way that they read out in an article, now that they experience it.

Sandy and Tony was a different kind of couple. They couldn't stay away from each other. Possible having someone else kept their marriage flowing. Two weeks after the party Roger, Sandy's old flame, introduced his family to Sandy and Tony. Sandy invited them to dinner. Roger, his girlfriend or common law wife and both kids. Roger's girlfriend was Hispanic and the children were seven and four respectfully. Roger's girlfriend was also sporting an engagement ring. Her name was Morrisa. She started telling Sandy and Tony that they have been together from she was sixteen years old, and that Roger was a good man, who loved his kids and her a lot. Sandy replied, true love is hard to find honey and when you find the right one, hold him tight and never let him get away honey. Tony and I have been through a lot and we love each other. Then she asked Roger when the wedding was. He replied as soon as we settle in Florida, and you guys will be coming down for it. Sandy, we wouldn't miss it for the world. About 8:00pm they left for home. Roger and Sandy kissed for the last time. She became very emotional and started crying, then she said I love you man, Thanks for the good times at work and take care of that lovely family you have. Roger reminded her to send pictures whenever they had their first child. Off into the sunset Roger went with good and bad memories, missing but not forgotten.

Kash and Uriel moved in together, he waited no longer, the vacuum salesman learned his lesson well. He realized that Kash was the one for him. He started working in the fiancé business at one stage Kash was pregnant but she had a miscarriage and was really sad. But they stuck together moved into a bigger apartment and started planning their wedding date. They still hung out together but Kash wasn't going to cheat anymore. She wanted a man for herself and didn't plan to share her man with anyone after her experience with Tony. She spent four years of her life waiting for a man that wasn't going to be hers. She had learnt a lot from Sandy of how to make her man happy sexually and in other ways. She plans to keep Uriel on cloud nine all year round. Uriel really loved Kash but couldn't get Vohn off his mind. After Vohn got married she and her husband moved to outer state to New Jersey then they both corresponded by phone.

Six months later Kaisha and Uriel finally got married. Sandy was her bridesmaid and Tony was the best man, great wedding and they honeymooned in the Bahamas. They had a small problem; you see Uriel's ex-girlfriend was pregnant when they broke up. She has the kid and Kash knew about it but didn't tell anyone. They both agreed the kids could visit anytime. Kash's parents didn't really like Uriel at first but after the wedding they became one happy family.

Now that the group had broken up, kash and Uriel got married. Roger and Marissa moved to Florida so Tony and Sandy looked to child bearing to stop their cheating ways. Sandy is the going out kind of girl and her groupies were leaving her. Although she and Kash worked at the same place and saw each other every day, and shared stories, Kash wasn't hanging out anymore that much. Just lunch and dinner, not much partying to Sandy had new groupies because she loved to party and meet new people.

Tony wasn't seeing anyone since Kash, it was hard to get over her. But there was this hot blonde and whenever he visited Sandy's office they made eye contact. Sandy had this young stockbroker that was crazy about her although he was married. Sean was English and men especially the white ones love a fine black woman.

Chapter 8

The New Beginning

Will Sandy And Tony Stop Cheating?

Cheating to most people is wrong because it makes and breaks the relationship. To Sandy and Tony, it strengthened and made their relationship better in every way. So is cheating good or bad? Sandy says cheating with respect to the other is an illusion make out live exotic. As long as we both don't know. This is an opinion to some but a reality to me says Sandy.

The great friendships of the past with Kasia and Tony and Sandy and Roger have ended. Intimately but she and Sandy remain co-worker and friends. After a couple of weeks the friendship with Sandy and the stockbroker started to get more serious/ They started going out a lot together. They even went away for a long weekend. Sandy mentioned to Kashia if she wanted to spend the weekend away so Kashia agreed and said that she would mention it to Uriel, but said don't tell Uriel. I am going out with Sean the stockbroker. Kashia says no way I am not going anywhere anymore without Uriel. We are living together and I will never disrespect him like that. Then Sandy says tell him that the girls are going out but for the weekend. She insisted but Kashia still said no. Then she said Sean and I have already booked the hotel, so you have got to help me. If Tony ask you why you didn't travel with us tell him Uriel had already made other plans. She went home that Wednesday night after having a couple of drinks with Sean. Tony wasn't home so she made herself sexy call tony on the cell phone to find out if he wanted dinner. It was about 10:30pm that night and at this time Tony was at work but he had already eaten dinner. So he said honey don't worry I just ordered and ate some Chinese food. She replied "honey I just had my bath and was thinking about you. That made me so horny. Honey I want you, I know we gonna make that baby tonight because I want you so bad. Wake me if I am sleeping ok. Honey you know that I could never refuse you. I love you honey. See you in a few. Tony got home about 12:30am because he called the blonde he likes to stop by her house for an hour to have a drink before he got home. Neither had made love yet because they had just met.

Anyway Tony gets home and as he entered the house he could smell the sweet smell of his wife. I want you honey he heard coming from the bedroom. He took his shower and entered the room. His wife was smiling and said thought I was sleeping? You know I don't go to bed until I get all of you. Before the love making began, they talked about how their love life has been great so far and how a lot of couples are complaining that after marriage how their love life has changed. But honey you noticed our love and feelings for each other has been the same since we met. You know why, because we love each other and when we are together there is no one else. Tony you are so right. We are special together, honey you need a glass of wine. Sandy sure baby and get the massage oil out. I have to give my baby a massage. He has been working so hard lately. So they drank the wine and she began to massage him. Then she said "I forgot to tell you, one of our clients bought a house in south jersey and invited some of us from the office. Can I go. You know I hate going out without you". Tony replied "honey you know we are not insecure with each other. If you want to go with your friends, that is ok with me. She replied "we will be sleeping over at a nearby hotel until Sunday afternoon. That's ok babe so they do the deed after the massage and then both cheaters went to bed.

Early in the morning, Tony went jogging to wake up his blonde princess. He told her that he was going to be alone for the weekend so that they can get together. She stated finally you can spend the night at my place so we can get to know each other better. She said "you know how long I have been waiting for this chance. I have something planed for you, you sexy man.

Sandy told Kashia that if she sees Tony and he asked her why she didn't go, tell him that Uriel had made previous plans. Anyway on Thursday, Sandy talked with Sean and told him everything was ok for the trip and that she was looking forward to it so they can have a great time together. Only to hear from Sean that he haven't told his wife about the trip yet. So that night Sean went home and took his wife some dinner. He was about to tell her about the trip but before he could mention it, she said "oh honey I almost forgot to tell you, mommy and daddy are on their way here from North Carolina to spend the weekend with us. Mom told me that daddy wants to surprise us. Guess who is coming too? My younger sister you haven't met. Remember she lived in California. She is just dying to meet you the boys. "But honey, I was planning to go to Jersey with the boys". "Honey you have to cancel that. My family will be upset if you are not here. Change your plans for next week. So he went to the bathroom and called Sandy to tell her there weekend plans have to be cancelled because his in-laws were coming in town. Remember that she already made plans and told her husband. Tony doesn't really have to change plans with his girl because she likes in _____ but have to find a way to stay out all night, As plan with her so that evening tony met with his girlfriend to plan the night.

After he reached home, he was home first and sandy came in about two hours later. Hi honey you are home early tonight. No late night at the office tonight"? "Not tonight I want to spend some quality time with you knowing, that you are going away,

for the weekend. Besides you know we are trying to make little Anthony. He laughed honey you are so funny. Sandy giggled after getting the news from Sean that the trip was off, she had to go to plan B. They had a shower together, massaged each other and then made love. Then Sandy says "honey this is so good that I don't want to leave for the weekend. I really enjoy trying to make this baby. I think we should make love all weekend long. Then Tony said that does ok go and have fun with your friends. The boys and I had planned to hang out knowing you will be away and I am the driver this week. She replied no problem honey. You can go out with your friends and I will stay home and relax this weekend. So, Tony' date was still on with the blonde girl. Her name was Leah. So the weekend was here and Sandy called Kashia to tell her she changed her mind and was staying home so she doesn't need an alibi. Kashia said that she and Uriel were going to this Jamaican club named Carib to dance Reggae. You can come with us ok. Girl I hope Uriel can handle four beauties. He is that good. Sandy, you didn't tell me that he ws good. In bed honey, have you ever heard of a Jamaican that was not good in bed. Bob Marley says "No Woman NO Cry" and they have the big bamboo hear what I say girl. He is the best! Ok ok, stop boasting. You asked so I am telling you, Uriel Hutch is the best.

So Saturday night came around and Tony left the house around 8:30pm to pick up Leah. They planned on having dinner. Sandy told Tony she was going out with Uriel and Kashia. They were going to a Jamaican club but she wasn't leaving until around 10:30pm because that was the time Jamaicans start partying. Have fun honey he kissed her and told her "later girl wa a gwan girl . . . that's a Jamaican phrase.

So Tony picked up Leah. It was their first real date. He took her to this French restaurant in midtown, the best French restaurant in Manhattan. The chef Jean Jorge was very nice. Leah said "I heard about this restaurant but I have never been here. "Honey, the food was marvelous Tony. You know I think I am falling for you. Last night after we talked, I lay down and you were there in bed with me. Every turn I made, you were there for me Mr. handsome Blackman. You know you are the first Blackman I ever dated. I have been missing a lot. They say once you go black you can't go back, so Mr. Tony I promise you I will stay. They just finished their first bottle of wine and she was already drunk. Tony had plans to go clubbing but after dinner she told him she didn't want to go to a club. She told him, "I want you tonight". "I want to spend the whole night with you. Do you think you can handle this"? She showed him her breast.

Into the second bottle of wine, Tony said "honey, I will try my best". She took out the other breast. "These are both yours tonight big boy", she whispered softly to him. She was now drunk and ready to leave. He took her home and they opened another bottle of wine. She went to the bath to take a shower and came out in this black negligee. Tony said "baby you are so beautiful, can I take a shower too". She replied "Yes T.B." (She called him T.B. Let me see what you come out in. Tony took his shower and came out with a towel wrapped around his waist. She came over to him and took his towel away. She said "damn, I want all of that tonight"!

So the show began and on and on it went. They never realized it was 7:30 Sunday morning. When he woke, he forgot he wasn't in his bed and that he was drunk. He would have to cook up an alibi to tell Sandy why he hasn't come home last night. So he called home while Leah was sleeping. He told Sandy that after he had dropped off the boys he was so drunk the cops was on the highway spot check with a breathalyzer, so he stopped at a motel and slept. He just woke up and he was on his way home. She told him "ok honey, I got home about an hour ago. I had a great time. I love you. See you babe, I'm going back to sleep". So Tony was happy and he went back to sleep for another hour.

When he woke up, he told Leah that he had a great time. She replied "I love you T.B. You make me feel brand new. Will I see you later"? Tony said "I will try". He put on his clothes and went home to Sandy. When he reached he called out to his wife. "Sandy honey, come here", but she was sleeping in the nude ready for action. I need my morning stuff baby. Give it to me please Tony. Tony was tired but he had to satisfy his wife. "honey, that Jamaican rum with coke made me hot. Cool me off, please cool me off" she begged. Afterwards, they both fell asleep and didn't wake up till 2:30 in the afternoon. That afternoon, they showered and then went out to dinner. Tony checked his cell phone and saw that Leah had called four times. While dinner was being served, he went to the bathroom and called her. She asked him where he was and he told her that he was having dinner with Sandy. She told him "I miss you, last night was so good, will I see you later T.B"? He told her "I will try but I have to go, bye, I love you". Back at dinner, Sandy was telling him about her first Jamaican party and how they danced reggae. Uriel was teaching Kashia and how she thought Uriel and Kashia looked good together. She said "they look just like us when we first started dating". Just then her phone rang. It was her boyfriend checking on her. He also sent her a text message wanting to see her later. When Tony asked who that was she told him "Kashia wants me to come over for dinner". He asked her "are you going"? she replied "yes but I won't eat". Tony smiled slyly to himself knowing that he would get another chance to see Leah again. So Sandy left, and planned to meet Sean at this special love nest by the Hudson River on 94th street. She told him "you can sit in your care or by the water looking over to New Jersey". Very romantic he told her. When they met, Sean asked her "have you ever been here before. She told him "yes, this is where Tony and I met. This was our special spot. It's great to relax especially on Sunday afternoon". "How did you make out on Saturday", he asked her. "I hope that I did not get you into trouble". She told him "no, Kashia and I went to this Jamaican spot and we had a great time". She asked him how was his in-laws. He told her "the same, I would have had more fun with you, but things happened sometimes for a purpose because if it wasn't for that, I wouldn't know this place we can hang out from time to time. I just love the view and the smell of your perfume. I love your cologne. I really like you a lot. God, why couldn't I have found you years ago? When, I was looking well.

Here I am now honey, please take me. You see I love you more than this because we will never get tired of each other. Everyday becomes a new day. We will never get tired of seeing each other. We can only see each other when we can and everyday I have learned that seeing each other every day depreciate the love and affection we have. Have you ever heard of the phrase absence makes the heart grow fonder? Well that's us. You tired of seeing your spouse because he is there day and night. It's not that you don't love each other but it's like a new flavor of ice cream. You always want to tast it and the first time you taste it you always want more. But if you get too much of it, you get a little tired of it. That's the way we have is and with that it keeps the love for Tony refreshing. You are never afraid to try the stuff. You learn from the other person with your spouse every time you try something with your spouse it makes you appreciate each other more and more. Sean you are such a beautiful person. The things you say is so true and so real that when you spend time with you it's cheating but it seems as if you have nothing wrong whenever you go home. You are so happy it makes everybody happy all daylong. You sometimes when I go home my honey ask me Sean why are you so happy and I would say honey that's the reason why I married you. You make me so happy when I am around you, that's what you are to me. I must confess I have never met a woman with such charisma and affection like you. Never and I have cheated before. Sandy honey never think of it as cheating. Call it sampling. Adam and Eve were put here to make each other happy and happiness doesn't grow on trees. In other countries people especially in Arabia men have four and five wives. In Utah the Mormons have six wives. In our world we can't only have one, but if we given the change to have more than one spouse we would just as bored. We would sleep with a different person every day. And we be just as bored as having one. Honey what I am saying is I don't see you every day. And whenever we meet and kiss and hug it's a brand new day. Sean to Sandy you are an amazing woman and I love you. Sean this was great Sandy, everything I will cherish and never forget.

It was really special to me and I hope this special (ice-cream?) flavor will always taste great. The evening was over. He dropped her off at her car; she stopped by Uriel and Kash before heading home. She called Tony from Kash phone so he could see her number on his cell. He answered "hi honey, say hi to Kash and Uriel for me. I'll be home later". One thing was that they never hanged up on each other without saying that they love each other, never! So, Tony knew where Sandy was and he called Leah telling her that he would be over. In fifteen minutes, he jumped into a cab and off to Leah he went. At the store he got something to drink. She was surprised when she opened the door. "You are here already. I was just fixing something to eat. Did you have dinner yet? "no" he answered. Well we will eat together then. She had nothing on. Tony said to her "honey, you are naked". You notice huh. When you said that you'll be over shortly I took my bath and decided to stay this way. It's easier to make love this way. I want us to have dinner and make love in the nude on the floor. I want you to be totally relaxed while we are together. You only spend a short time and during your stay I want all of your attention every minute of it". So she made dinner and grabbed a bottle of wine, slipped in a video of porn of course. Tony said "we are lucky to have each other. Before the word came out his mouth, she was all over him. "Honey", she moaned. I can't get enough of you. Last night was great but right now is better. They didn't start eating until an hour later. They drank all the wine before they ate the dinner.

While they ate they talked about were their relationship was going. He turned to her and said "Sandy and I have been together for about 6 years and married for 5. But she never let me feel the way you make me feel. Honey you are such a great lover. My affairs with you are the best I ever had. Leah told him "you are the fourth man I've been to bed with. I had a boyfriend in college. He was ok and he was the one that took my virginity. So I love him but he loved someone else. I told myself that I will never fall in love again. Then you came into my life. As I was thinking after you left last night, I said to" myself" "why are you dating a married man? But none of my ex-boyfriend's stimulates and let me feel this good. And you are the first black man I ever made love to. I always here you guys were great. Well it's been proven to me so I don't care if you are married. Just try to "see me at least three times per week and I will be happy. I don't need your money I make a lot. All I need is you whenever you can. Then Tony told her "Sandy, my wife and I are trying to have a kid for the past year. We are still trying but nothing and don't worry no one can keep me away from seeing you. I promise to see you as often as I can".

Honey, Leah says although you are married you are my fulltime. I don't another and I will be always here for you. In fact, I will give you the keys to my apartment tomorrow. They cuddled and kissed. It was about 8pm, then he left, reached home and Sandy was home already. "Sandy, honey you are home early tonight". You know there's a lot on my mind. I love being home early you know we're trying to make that baby and that means more sex for me. There is nothing I love more than making lovely love to you. Each time it's like the first time. Honey you got that right. That's how a marriage couple should do it and there will never be any cheating in this relationship.

Many couples don't know the real art of love making. Honey I must confess you are the man. Turn the lights down low, Tony. They attacked each other, then went to sleep. They went to sleep with smiles on there faces. Tony last words were "there is so much fun making this baby. Good night.

Chapter 9

Sandy and Kash made plans to get pregnant the same year. Although Kash wasn't married, they always discussed how hard they were going to try to get it done. The only difference was that Sandy was screwing with Sean her boyfriend and Kash was only sleeping with Uriel.

It was Monday morning July 11th. The sun came up about 6:30am that morning. Tony and Sandy woke up to take their shower and get ready for work. Sandy called Kash and told her she would be a little late and how she had a great night last night. "Me too", Kash replied. "In fact we are doing it now, that Uriel is one sex maniac. He turned me into an animal girl. Girl I am too tired. Tony did work me oer too. Anyway see you at the office. We will chat".

Off to work Tony went leaving Sandy getting dressed. As the car drove off, she couldn't wait to call Sean to find out how his weekend went. They talked about missing each other's company and how much they loved each other. And that they would meet for lunch. On the way to work, Tony called Leah and they talked about spending the night thinking about him and how much a great lover he is. She brought out her vibrator but it wasn't the same. She missed his soft lips all over her body. She smiled and told him "honey, from now on my vibrator's name is Tony Jr. He can't replace you but he will keep me busy and thinking of you. He dropped her off at work; they kissed and made plans to see each other later. You see Leah knows that Tony was trying to make this baby and was having a lot of sex with his wife. So she would make love to him and send him home ready.

Both Sandy and Tony's relationship was secured although they were doing someone else on the side. Leah didn't want to kid, she was on birth control. Sandy was doing Sean but he didn't use a condom. He was half white and Tony was black. Kash was a Uriel girl. She loved him so much.

After about a month passed, Kash called Sandy to tell her that she was late with her period. Sandy told Kash that she was also late, but didn't want a false alarm. She said "I want to make sure I'm pregnant before telling Tony. You know how excited he would get". Kash said "yes I know girl". A month passed and both girls decided to go to the drug store and buy a pregnancy test. They both the tests the same night and both girls came out positive. They were so happy, they started jumping up and down screaming at each other. Then there was a pause. Kash asked Sandy "why did you get so quiet?" Sandy answered "I am in trouble. Sean and I have never used a condom. Suppose the baby is his child and comes out with his complexion? What do I tell Tony? Kash told her "don't worry about it. That kid is Tony's". They both decided to tell their partners until they were absolutely sure they were pregnant. But it would make both men happy. They waited until another two weeks and they still didn't have their periods. They both talked a lot over lunch and especially Kash. She was so happy he wanted to have Uriel's kid so bad. It was the same with Sandy. She was having unprotected sex with her boyfriend Sean. One evening they were having dinner. Suddenly she said to Sean "you know I love you. And you know we both are seeing someone else. When we make love you don't use a condom, have it ever run through your mind that I might get pregnant? If that happens what would you do, she asked him. He replies "honey, we will cross that bridge when we get there. Sandy told him "honey I am serious. How would I know if it is yours or Tony's. He replied "honey you know I will stand by you. "So what do I do about my husband Sean". Time passed and he did not answer her question. She asked him "would you leave your relationship to be with me Sean?" "Honey you are ruining dinner with all this negative talk. Then she says "Sean I have bad news. I missed my period last month and I did a pregnancy test. The test came up positive. I haven't even mentioned this to my husband Tony. I told you first, but I don't think that it's nothing to be nervous about. Kash and I are going to see our doctor tomorrow". Then she told Sean that the joke how she and Kash had hoped that they could get pregnant together and now they are both pregnant. Sean asked her "are you really pregnant? Are you going to have our baby?" "yes I will" Sandy whispered. "it depends on who the baby looks like, you or Tony". "You are funny, that's why I love you", Sean said laughing at her.

During dinner she called Tony so see if he was working late so she can spend more time with Sean. Then Sean called his house to say he was going to be late. Tony picked up and told Sandy that he should be home by 10:30pm that night. Then Sandy replied "honey, I have great great news". "What he asked"? "Honey please, tell me, I hate surprises. No honey you have to wait until I get home. Your dream has come true. Honey, don't tell me you won the lotto. Now I can get that BMW I always wanted. This is better than the lotto. Honey, wait until you get home. After, hanging up, Tony called Leah, honey I'm coming over with a bottle of champagne. We gonna celebrate baby! Leah got suspicious. "Babe what are we going to celebrate. Oh, my love for you? I can't wait to get you. Youv'e been on my mind since I left you this morning.

Tony Leah "honey did I tell you I love you this morning. If I didn't I am sorry. I really love you so much, I really do. Ok baby. She replied "honey I will be here waiting for you when you get home. Then you can tell me how much you love me. About 6:30pm Tony pulled up and rang her bell. He had to be home by 10pm. He left his cell phone in the car so as not to be disturbed by anyone. His beautiful Leah comes out in a red and white negligee very short. You could smell her fragrance a mile away. They kissed. Tony honey I really, really love you she replied I know babe. She took the bottle and put it in the freezer. She directed him to the bathroom where his bath was set with various on top of the suds. She took his clothes off and laid him down and started to bathe him. five minutes after, they were both in the tub taking each other apart. They went to the bedroom and the rest of the evening was astonishing romantics.

Isn't romance beautiful and sexy when you are with the other woman? The only difference with this relationship his wife give him the love and passion and ecstasy like his girlfriend does.

They drank the bottle of champagne and about 10pm Tony had to leave. He called home from Leah's phone. He knows there is no caller ID. He told Sandy he is on his way. "great honey" she replied. "I made a light dinner and your bath is set". While he was talking to Sandy, his girlfriend Leah was putting the glasses they drunk out of away. She never really listened to Tony when he was on the phone with his wife. She respected his marriage. She would like him all for herself but will never tell him to leave his wife for her. She enjoyed being number two. They kissed and he told her "goodbye" see you tomorrow morning. I will pick you up for work in the morning". As Tony drive up to his condo, he called Leah to tell her he is home and that he loved her.

As he opened the door, there was his lovely wife of 5 years in a black negligee with very thin straps about the knee. They ran into each other's arms kissing and telling each other how they loved each other. She kept kissing her husband all over. None of them had any guilty feelings about seeing someone else.

She undressed like Leah does and put him in the tub to bathe him. She dried him off and put massage lotion all over him. They sat for dinner with a drink of wine. He was ready for the great news. They she told him "honey, you are my Mandingo. I love you so much. Life would be nothing without you. I knew we could do it. Guess what? We are having a baby, we are having a baby!! "What are you talking about" Tony asked her. She answered "I haven't seen my period, I am two weeks late and guess what again. Kash and Uriel are having a baby too. How do you know that? We were planning parenthood together. Tony replied "are you sure honey that this isn't a false alarm." "Well we took the pregnancy test at the drug store and it showed that we are pregnant. So we made an appointment with our doctor for next week to make sure. Tony was so happy, honey I hope we have a son. Honey does it really matter what we have. I first want a baby ok. Tony replied ok. The phone rang. It was Kash. Honey child great news. I told Tony aout our having a baby and he said he doesn't want his child to be born out of wedlock. So he brought home an engagement ring. He said if I am really pregnant we will get married before the kids is born. If not, then we will do it in June of next year. Sandy told Tony they both congratulate both of their engagement and planned to party harty over the weekend after they both visited the doctor.

So on Wednesday the two princesses visited their doctor after work. They did there test and the doctor came out later smiling great news gals. You are both six weeks pregnant. Great timing are you sure you girls don't sleep with the same guy jokingly. Sandy replied "I wish". Dr. ok girls I was just joking. Both ladies hugged and kissed each other for joy. There was a little silence on Kash part when the doctor said that.

Knowing that she was sleeping with Tony for a long time but she pick up herself. They both called their spouses and then these guys were happy especially Kash because she genuinely loved Uriel. For the past six years before she met Uriel she only slept with her best friend husband. It meant a lot to her that that they were both pregnant.

Tony wanted to tell his girlfriend Leah about it but was relationship. So after knowing that his wife was really pregnant he became a little tense whenever he visited Leah. She realized there was something bothering him. He wasn't as happy as before. One evening Leah asked him "baby, are you having a problem at home? Lately you've not been your old sweet self". He replied "It's nothing. It's just that I am having a problem with this client at work and a little pressure from the boss man, but otherwise I love you". Leah told him "come on Tony you and I have been together for too long. Cut out the bullshit and be honest with me. Listen; there is nothing that can keep us apart. Even, if your wife caught us. I am not leaving you. Not now, not then. We are bind together. You see Tony you are the only guy who treats me with respect and love and I've been around a lot of single losers. You are the first married man I ever talk to and love. It is because of your honest the first time we met.

I was brought up and my mom and dad told me never to get involved with a married man because I will be hurting the other woman. More over I will always be number two. She also said "married men will never leave their wives for number two, but I've dated single men for a long time and sometimes I was number five. Not two, not three, but five! So I decided to settle right now for number two. You know why? Because when you are not here I know where you are, and when you leave you leave me with a smile on my face. I don't love you for money, I make money. You are my lover, my friend, my everything. So tell me what's bothering you babe. Then Tony told her "ok. You forced it out of me. I am pregnant, and I am not sure it's your baby. Honey I always tell you not to stay on top too long but you wouldn't listen. Now I am having your baby. That was so funny, funny man! They hugged, kissed, laughed and screamed. Then she said to him "that's what this is all about? Your wife is pregnant. That's great news! You guys have been together for so long. It's about time! Mr. Sexman you so good you make both of us happy. I am so lucky to be apart of this. And I love it. How far along is she? Tony answered "she is about six weeks the doctor says. Then he says honey nothing will stop us being together because when I am down, I just have to look at your face and body and we both stands up. Thanks for understanding me.

Well, it was the weekend and Kash, Sandy, Uriel, and Tony planned to celebrate on Saturday night. Kash wanted to go to the same club where she met Uriel the vacuum salesman. She was glad that she did not chose the financial banker. Her Uriel give her a lot of attention and she loved him. That Friday evening, Sandy called Tony and told him she was gonna celebrate with the girls for a couple of hours. "No problem honey" Tony replied. Sandy called Sean so they can meet. Sean wanted seafood and he knew this place in Brooklyn that have fresh fish. So off to Brooklyn they went. Leah cooked one of her special meals for Tony. All he had to do was bring the wine.

On the trip to Brooklyn, Sandy and Sean talked about the possibility of the kid being his. "Sean it is possible. We have never used contraceptives" Sandy told him. He replied "we will cross that river when we get there" She said "Sean do you really love me. Suppose after the kid is born it looks like you. Then Tony kicks me out. Would you leave your girlfriend for me? Honey I will if you leave and swimming is the way to get to you. I can't swim but I will always be there for you. See, when I'm with you I can't help myself. I really love you. If you weren't married I would have left her already. I am so happy around you sometimes I'm at home and I am so unhappy. I just think about you and I instantly get positive. I don't see you as married, I see you as the love of my life.

Chapter 10

Notes on Chapter 10

*A*fter three months of being pregnant, Sandy had a miscarriage. *Kashia also fell in the house and started to bleed. Her neighbor took her to the hospital. Uriel was at a conference. She also lost her child. Sandy decided to take a break and go on a vacation alone. She told Tony she would "be good for them". Tony did the same and went on vacation to Jamaica. He took Leah with him. Sandy also went with Sean on her vacation. The couple corresponds a lot by cell phone. Sean told his girlfriend he was going on a business trip.*

Three months have passed and Sandy and Kashia were making preparation to be new mothers. During that time they had this big party at the club where Uriel and Kash met. Well the party was not really that big with guests, was big because of its important, two new kids was coming into the world and the mothers and fathers were happy. The guests was mostly regulars and well wishers, together there everyone had a great time then Kash showed off her engagement ring to the group, everyone was happy for her and they all congratulate the new mothers with hugs and kisses.

A month later one night, Sandy woke up and found her bed all mess up. Tony thought there was nothing wrong, Tony took her to the hospital, she was there for a couple of hours, the doctor then came out with sad news to Tony, "Sir it's really hard to tell you this, but your wife just had a miscarriage", 'damn' cried Tony, "how could that happen, we've been waiting so long to have this child." Tony was really sad about the miscarriage, he and Sandy been trying for about four years. The doctor told hi, he can see his wife now, he went in and show his disappointment, his wife cheer him up, "Honey don't worry we can do this all over again, I am still young and you know how much fun we had trying, it's going to be more fun trying again, you know why, because we're going to try harder and harder until I'm pregnant again, ok, Honey I love you so much." Tony stayed for a while then he leave. The doctor want to keep her overnight because she bleed so much, shortly after Tony leave she called Kash and give her the sad news, Kash get really emotional for her, knowing how badly they both plan to have kids together, then Sandy said to Kash "Honey you told the fourth you know I am going to be a God-mother and I am going to love it too. Then she called Sean to give him the news, Sandy to Sean "hi Honey it's a sad day in our life," Sean "what is it Honey? What happen to you don't tell me you had an accident are you in the hospital, are there any broken bones and he went on and on, then she says get a hold of yourself damn it I'm in the hospital it's an accident but not a car accident I had a miscarriage and we lost our child, Sean oh Honey I am so sorry real sorry to hear you lost our baby, but we won't stop until we do it again any way what did your husband say? He was devastated real sad about it but he will get over it. Things happen for a reason. To be honest, we wouldn't know how this child would turn out, I didn't know whose it was yours or his so you know you have to start using condoms or some method, I am not going to stop seeing you never but if I should get pregnant again, I want to positively share who kid it is right baby, and you know you are my little smukums and I love you Sean.

Honey can I come visit you in the hospital no honey that's cutting it close lets keep our love the way it is Tony, Kash and Uriel visited, they bought flowers and candy they had big laughs Tony talked about wait until you get home honey you going to be pregnant again by next week ok my funny man Sandy laugh ok we will see she had to stay over another night so they leave her about 8"30pm. Uriel and his fiancee left and Tony went to see his precious Leah, she ask about her Tony say she will be out in another day so lets go get something to eat.

It's early on the way to the restaurant Leah mentioned it was sad about your wife miscarriage sometimes I think when you date married men like I do you get a little nervous when there child around because you see less of the man he have more responsibility to his family Tony honey you know I would be like that you are my sun in the morning you are my lunch at noon you are the glare of the sunlight when it goes down you are moon in the nighttime most of all you are the love of my life no matter what season we bring you are everything I ever wanted being married don't stop you from being number 1.

Leah, so baby when your wife coming home tomorrow afternoon her friend and I are going to pick her up anyway baby lets concentrate on us tonight after dinner Tony call his wife telling her he is a little depress and he is at the bar so he will be home late he cover all bases so there no slip up he spend all night with Leah never leave until 3pm, you are the one I wish things could be like this for a lifetime you are so special, Tony you don't have to worry I am going nowhere not now not then Leah honey I know bye see you tomorrow.

The following day Sandy was discharge from the hospital before Tony leave work to pick her up there was a surprise guess who Sean surprise her after their hugging and kissing she instantly call Tony tell him he don't have to be there until after 5pm so he should keep his cell phone she will call him after she do her final test all she was doing was buying more time to spend with Sean she haven't see Sean for a while so they was all over each other in the hospital at one stage the Head nurse came in and saw Sean there she ask Sandy is this your husband, I haven't met him she haven't see Sean for a while so they was all over each other in the hospital at one stage the Head nurse came in and saw Sean there she ask Sandy is this your husband, I haven't met him such a fine gentle man she say no Miss Smith this is my cousin Danny nice to meet Sir she will be out today Sir such a beautiful lady thanks. Shortly after the nurse left her doctor gave her the ok that she can go home today but should be careful don't harass herself and he will see her in two weeks for her check-up being she can start on baby number two and she cannot have sex until the prescription is finished, ok doc I will do just fine thanks Sean help her pack and leave downstairs to the Lobby there Sean stay with her until Tony gets there so for the first time both men met they shake hands then Sandy introduce him as an old friend who used to work for her company then relocated he call the office and the girl told him I was in the hospital so he came to visit, so as Sean leave Sandy yell give my love to your wife and kids, knowing he isn't married but she cover all bases great to meet you that Tony so off home they went. Has she reach home she was surprise to see Kash and her coworkers there they bought her flowers they also had a little welcome home party order sandwiches in one friend bought her a surprise gift a box of durex condoms she open it and says whoever brought this can have it because my husband going to do it four times a night to make sure the next one stays right honey correct dear in fact we're going to start tonight the doctor we said we have to wait until about three weeks he gave me some tonic so after this finish I'm going to screw your brains out.

The group was in ecstasy that was real funny Sandy. Miss Kash is pushing down the place with her fat stomach Tony you see when Uriel do it stay not like you Honey I love you anyway they had a great evening it was the weekend and Sandy was a little drug up so the guest left Kash say Uriel have to work tomorrow so the little welcome home was over, you see Sandy was the live wire in the office about 10:30 next day it was Saturday Kash call to see how Sandy was doing Tony answer and say she was sleeping then Kash says she was cleaning up, Uriel left early Kash see you guys later Tony get up clean up the house because he knows about midday most of Sandy friends coming over she woke up but before he call his princess Leah they talk and talk then ask babe will I see you later he reply honey you know have kiss those beautiful lips everyday to keep them moist and fresh of coarse you'll see me later then the house phone rang he pick up it was Sean good morning Sir just checking how your wife is she is fine do you want to talk to her hold a minute Tony honey I hear you shuffling are you yes who is it honey it's Sean ok I I'll pick up honey I got it, this is getting dangerous Sean says with me call your home not that's ok, Tony is very understanding but when I am better we go back to our cell phones little did they know Tony had the love of his life on didn't care a shit he trust his wife and there was no insecurity with these two. About 1:30pm Sandy get a call check the caller id, it says "Hospital" she check because she taught it was Sean, but it was Uriel "Man I am in big shit here" Kash feel on the vacuum while cleaning and start bleeding all over the place, she is in intensive care, she is bleeding like hell she is going to lose the baby, man this is serious and I told he had to leave the cleaning to me with that heavy Kirby man. I hope she come through I really love that woman; he was crying she was the best thing that ever happen to me. I can't afford to lose her, no way man no way. Sandy be calm she going to be ok God is looking over her for us she will pull through. Tony was listening he also was crying, Sandy to Tony "Oh my pooh pooh you're crying" "yes she was our best friend with Sandy, no knowing she and Tony had a thing going. Tony still cares for her; she was always there for them. Uriel says the doctor say no guess until she is ok only family, bye until, talk to guys when those pills they gave her wore off. Love you guys Sandy we will pray for her anything Uriel please call us ok?"

Then Sandy call in her pooh pooh Tony stop crying she will be ok she is like family; she was with us from the beginning. She hugs her and they became silent for a while then they have breakfast.

It was a really bad month for these two young couples but they will get over two days later Kash doctor decide she was well enough to have visitors so the whole gang went from the office, she was well but she was lonely she miss her friends and her Uriel so Sandy and the gang went they wheel her out in a chair the doctor says she is lucky to be alive.

What save he she is a strong lady, then Uriel start to tell his story about hoe he lost his mother and sister in child's birth, he at one time think he was curse. All the people that he loves was dying the same way and he was glad Kash survive, that means the curse is gone, he can't afford to lose another love one this way, it was a real sad moment to hear a grown man spill his guts to the people around him, but he was happy she was well or getting well again. Anyway everyone turn the sad moment into . . . . Ms. Sandy says Kash and I'm going back to the drawing board, they're going to try again and again and this time it's going to be right girl we going to have the two babies if it's the last thing we do, so you two boys better take your wheatees and be strong it going to take more and more. Mr. Uriel smile thanks guys you make me happy again, then he kissed his Kash two weeks, later she was home, her doctor also told her the reason she took so long to get pregnant, it's because she had fibroids they recommend her to a specialist who would take care of such during this time Tony, Sandy and Uriel starts planning their vacation, the boys vigor their ladies needs rest. Sandy and Tony decided if they take separate vacation it would be nice Kash and Uriel want to visit the nude beaches in Negril, Jamaica Sandy wants to visit Mexico and Tony Bahamas before Kash go on vacation she have her fibroids remove the specialist says it would only take a couple of hours and after they go on their vacation so Uriel and Kash bought tickets on Air Jamaica to Negril after the operation it would be done by laser, so it won't take long, Sandy and Tony have different vacation days so one would have to leave while the other stays, so while while Sandy leaving Tony will be at home alone with Leah while planning Uriel can take vacation anytime so there is no problem for Kash they already mode their reservation and plan to have the operation early morning the day before she leaves since it will take no time.

So two month later after Kash fully recover from her miscarraige she was ready to try while on vacation to get pregnant again. Kash and Sandy had plan that they are going to leave the same day she don't really want to leave before she is sure Kas, operation went well that how close they are so the big day arrive, Kash pack her and Uriel stuff in one bag head to the hospital the doctor was ready, later Sandy turn up Sandy and Uriel waited in the guess room, Tony went to work they both flying out the same airport an hour apart, so they waited and waited about two hours past there no news about Kash, they notice there was a lot of in and from the room where the operation was taken place so they got suspicious and for the doctor who doing the operation on Kash she came out. Tony and Sandy ask is there a problem she reply sir there is a big problem we had a big malfunction with the laser system it went too far and damage your wife's uterus and her kidney so now we have to do another operation because she has internal bleeding, there' nothing too serious, sir I will get back to you, Sandy reply are people f—ing professional how could you let this happen, do you know we are suppose to leave on vacation you said it was just a couple of hours.

Uriel was so stunned he was speechless he could believe his faith, Uriel call Sandy a cab about 1:30pm her flight to Mexico was 3:30pm, she made a call from the hospital to Sean he was on his way to the airport she mention what happen to Kasha she we have to talk on the plane see you horny then she call time telling there was a minor problem with Kash no detailing what happen only that was heading to the airport. Tony have fun honey call when you touch down and tell Kash and Uriel no forget to call me I will be home alone while you guys are frolicking on the beach. Sandy was off to the airport to meet Sean, Sean told his girlfriend he was on his way to Mexico on business trip which wasn't unusual he always go away on long trips even before he met Sandy.

Uriel and Kash was unable to take their vacation they been planning for she end up had to have major operation she was in the hospital for another week and then have to make regular visits. Sandy was back from vacation in Mexico and had to help Uriel with her, Uriel had to work, Tony and Leah went to Jamaica, Hendism in Negril they spend a week had a great time brought back a lot of picture had to leave at Leah house so Sandy couldn't get hold of them. Months after Kash operation she still feel pain, she and Uriel got married. They sued the hospital for a large sum of money, the hospitals settle the claims but in turn sue the laser company because it malfunction.

Chapter 11

Sandy and Tony continue seeing their outside lovers; Sean fell so much in love with Sandy he separated from his loving girlfriend because it was interesting with him seeing Sandy a lot. One weekend Sand and Sean went to the Poconos they rented this fancy weekend cottage with everything included indoor I mean one of the bedroom had a pool she called Tony on her cell phone and left line open and Tony overheard her talking to this man on the line the only thing they was talking like they were in a relationship so he hang up that was the closest she ever get in being caught when she realize her phone was hang up she freaks and was worried she got caught, so she call Tony and tried to find out if he hear her conversation, he say honey I heard you talking to a stranger you might hurt and always make you check your phone after a conversation, never leave your line open you never know who may be listening ok. Sandy I love you honey see you Sunday evening Tony never mind that she is because there is always Leah to make him happy.

90% of women think that only men cheat, but the ladies cheats equally, the only reason they never get caught is because they are more cleaver than men. If your wife goes out and cheats on you, you can never know unless someone tells you. All she have to do is to get home before you take her bath smells real good and as her husband enter the door make sure she has on his favorite fragrance set his bath make dinner or snacks kiss and caress him and always do this whenever she goes out with the other guy, he will never know as long as you continue to make him sexually happy even if you don't enjoy it pretend he is the only person can make you have three big orgasm in one night, if you do that every time you make love to him, he will never even suspect you and that's what Sandy was doing to Tonya lot of time, she fakes so hard. Tony would go in the bathroom and flex his muscles and say to himself how good he was, even though Sandy was faking, but men loves to be macho. You see Tony had two women, one who was faking and one who was for real the only reason Sandy was faking is to cover her track, not because Tony was good sexually but how many orgasm can a lady have in one night. Tony was a great lover when Sandy don't sleep with Sean very passionate wife loves her husband, if she didn't love him and the sex was bad she would have left him long ago, but the outside experience and the adventure of not being caught make her life exciting, very exciting.

Now on Tony' behalf, he find excitement even more exciting when he was dating Kashia, Sandy's friend, he feel like a _____ because he has the comfort of two beautiful friends whenever he wants even on his wedding night he had two brides, the bridesmaid Kashia his wife Sandy, what else can you ask for, you are higher than cloud nine you are in heaven and this relationship with Kashia went on for three years, two friends. If Kashia had break it off he would still be with her, she was pretty, sexy, good lover like his wife, he didn't miss anything at home because both ladies talk about how to make the man happy only that it was the same man they use the same perfume so if he goes home smelling like he left home in the morning she figures she was the last person he hug before work, now there's a difference with Leah she was Caucasian and use different fragrance from Sandy's so to keep the smell going he had to introduce Leah to this new perfume, they are of different nationality so she had to try it so when they first met the second date he bought her a gift a bottle at Victoria Secret, in fact he bought two to make sure the one at home doesn't run and his wife shift fragrance on him so again both ladies smells the same and his wife Sandy loves that fragrance because when she goes out with Sean and comes home she know Tony love that smell so Tony was back in business. Now you might say how does Tony service both ladies, sometimes and don't lose his erection and never fail in action, never gets tired, it's like playing soccer after the first ten minutes you get better and have more stamina, the more sex Tony have per night the better and longer he last, it's like ever ready batteries go on and on and on and on the same thing with the ladies, the more sex you get, the better you get.

I have interview about 150 soccer players, black, white and Hispanic and they all say their sex life gets better when they have a girlfriend on the side, whenever you have a fight at home then visit your girlfriend, she make you a cup of tea, make love to you that make you so happy you forget about how sad your wife make you that night, you go home with a smile on your face, you give your wife hugs and kisses and forget that you two had a fight.

The ladies say they have to be always the aggressor to her husband husbands loves when their wives are the aggressor because she wants him.

Will Tony and Sandy ever got caught, ever get caught? Uriel and Kashia had twins after she got well. Sandy and Tony never had kids but still doing what makes them happy.

Chapter 12

All of the wedding plans between Tianna and Sean were coming down to the finishing touches. Tianna and Sean's parents decided to meet up at the house of Tianna's parents. They were going to plan the date of the wedding.

Earlier that Sunday morning, Sean woke up Tia and said, "Today we are going to meet our family to plan the beginning of our great future together. If it was left to me, we would just stop by City Hall together one evening and tie the knot. We would be just as happy. But you know our parents have to stick to their tradition with this GREAT BIG BASH! I don't see the difference. We've been living together for about three years now." Tia simply sighed.

They got ready and headed to New Jersey. The announcements were going to take place at the Tia's parent's house, the Bruseburgs. Sean's parent's, the Brimsteins, were also going to New Jersey to make dinner arrangements for the wedding.

At 12:30, Sean and Tianna arrived. Sean's parents arrived an hour later. They brought a bottle of Kosher Wine and some appetizers. Around the living room, their faces were lit up with smiles and laughter filled the room. Everyone was in a great mood to get married and send Sean and Tianna on their happy journey to wedlock. Well after the fun and laughter toned down, Mr. Bruseburg and Mr. Brimstein went outside. Sean followed, leaving the ladies inside. Tia and her sisters went shopping leaving their parents alone. Mr.Bruseburg told Sean's father about his plans to make Sean a leading partner in his corporation and he wanted to get his opinion.

Mr. Brimstein replied, "That's a decision he has to make on his own. He already has experience in the field with the company he currently works for."

Sean calmly replied, "Yes Dad. I've been thinking about this for a while. I've even discussed this with Tia and she thinks it would be a great idea. And Mr. Bruse, I see you two have been communicating already. That's good".

The guys toasted to their agreement and went for a walk on the beach to talk about business; and the future of their joint venture between Sean and his future father-in-law. Meanwhile, Mrs.Bruseburg and Mrs.Brimstein agreed on a date for the wedding and later joined their husbands on the beach to discuss what they thought was best for the wedding. Sean asked to be excused so that he could tell his friends the great news.

The first person Sean called was his girlfriend, Sandy, to tell her the good news. She congratulated him and told him how happy she was with his decision. She joyfully exclaimed, "Tianna is a great lady". Sean replied, "I will tell you the date later when they announce it at the dinner table". He closed the conversation saying, "I love you".

It was Sunday and the weekend was coming to an end. Kashia, Sony and Sandy had a great weekend together. They watched a movie and went clubbing together. Their husbands were waiting for them. Kashia and Sandy went separated themselves from the pack to have a girl talk.

Kashia asked Sandy, "What happened to the white guy that you were hanging out with the night that I first met Uriel?" Sandy jovially replied, "We're still in contact with each other. We see each other all the time. As you know my ex-boyfriend left with his family to Florida from the night Sean and I met. Like I said, we have never stopped seeing each other. It's been two years to be exact. In fact, he was the person I was talking to on the phone a few minutes ago. He even sent his regards to you. Sean had a girlfriend this whole time".

Kashia raised her eyebrows in shock. Sandy continued by saying, "Yeah. They got engaged about six months ago. And today, they and their parents were making wedding plans. He decided it was time to tie the knot. He asked me what I thought and I told him to go for it as long as it doesn't affect his relationship. You see Kash, you have to be fair. I have been married the whole time and he still loves me. So why should I stand in his way? Nothing is going to change. Kash . . . honey, there is something so special about that man."

"Not really Sandy", said Kashia in a nonchalant tone. Kashia continues," You have always liked light skin or *browning* as you call them, just like Roger. You never really liked Uriel because he was dark skin *and* a vacuum cleaner salesman. You have always wanted a Wall Street type of guy. But honey, I am happy with a salesman. My man is making moves". Kashia smiled and Sandy smiled along with her. Kashia continued, "Oh, didn't I tell you? Uriel is working with Prudential, one of the largest insurance companies in the United States. He also has his stockbroker license".

"That's great Kash. I'm happy for you. You see . . . I admit I don't know everything about men. And oh, before I forget. Sean is inviting Tony and me to the wedding. I helped him pick out the engagement ring and he said he loved it". Kashia laughs and sarcastically belts out, "Hey, that's not fair!"

At that very moment, Kashia started to reflect on her life. Life is a funny thing. Before she met Uriel, she was dating Tony. Then she met Sandy, who became her best friend. She was even Sandy's Chief Bridesmaid when Sandy and Tony got married. How could she forget? Now she was the one telling her best friend what was right from wrong. It's really funny how people change, but true love can do that to you.

Kashia realized that she could forget the past, but she could make amends for the future; and the present. She had already done this when she met Tony, the love of her life. She asked God to forgive her for the mistakes she made in her past. She then hugged her friend Sandy and expressed how much she loved her.

Sandy told her, "I love you too. Please . . . be careful in what you do. Try not to lose Tony, because both of you have come a long way". Sandy replied, "Aw, thanks. You have been with me long enough. Tony is my husband and my life. Sean is just my lover. With him being married, he would only have time for his wife and himself. And you know you and I have been best friends for a long time. No one can come between us. And keep that progressive husband of yours happy. I am really sorry I disrespected your judgment of choosing a good man. You proved me wrong."

The union between these two best friends continued although they have their differences of opinion. Their weekend was great. Later that day, Uriel announced that he knew a great place in the Bronx. Sandy happily announced, "I hope its Jamaican food. That's what I feel like having today. And please Uriel; don't give Tony none of that Jamaican over proof that can't make *that thing* go down." They all laughed.

Uriel smiled and replied, "Well that might be just what I need tonight. We might even make the baby we have been looking for. Remember Kash? We both got pregnant just months apart last time. So girl, let's try it again!"

Kash said to Uriel sarcastically, "Where is that place?" He replied, "We have been there before. It's that go-go club we always go to on Boston Road., but we are going to dinner."

Tony joined the conversation saying, "It's a club and a restaurant now. I have never eaten there since it changed, but the boys tell me the food is great."

"Ok. Ok", Sandy replied.

They all packed themselves into a car and went to the club. Kashia was surprised because compared to the last time her and Tony were there, the club looked completely different.

Sandy shouted, "DAMN! This is beautiful", when she entered the club and restaurant duo.

The atmosphere was great. They eyed the jazz and piano bar as they were escorted to their table.

"This place is great. There is a television everywhere so that we can watch the games while we eat. Man, this is the life!"

The waiter came over and politely asked "Can I get any of you something to drink?"

Tony ordered a bottle of the finest wine and a shot of over proof rum on the side.

Sandy said, "Honey, you're drinking the over proof rum too early."

Tony replied, "Well honey, I'm getting ready when I hear the words 'baby making'."

At that very moment the champagne arrived, the band started playing and the girls ordered an appetizer to kick off the Sunday night.

Uriel scratched his head and said, "It seems like Jamaican ladies are getting very smart—no more cooking every Sunday like they're accustomed to. You go girls!"

Kashia pompously replied, "Uriel, people work too hard to cook every Sunday. But thanks honey; I'm glad you understand."

They poured the wine and champagne, and made a toast to good times and friendship forever. The band was playing one of Adele's songs, which was Uriel's favorite. He asked Kash for a dance. They danced while the other two love other love birds started to kiss.

Kashia said to Uriel, "That over proof started working already. After our dance I'll have one too honey but I'll wait until we're about to leave."

She kissed him passionately and said, "I love you Mr. Big Bamboo Man."

They went back to the table where the other two locked lips together. Suddenly, Tony's cell phone rang. Guess who? It was Leah, his princess and girlfriend. His wife said, "Honey, take your call quickly and tell your friend that we are at dinner."

"Okay honey, I will", replied Tony.

You see Tony generally spent Sundays with Leah. He had told her he was having company. Leah said "I know you're with your friends, but I am accustomed to having you make love to me at this time. So I am just calling to say I Love . . ." He interrupted and said "I love you too princess, call you later, bye."

On Monday morning, at 9:00, Tony secretly made his way over to Leah's house. Leah was happy to see him. He decided to call his wife, Sandy, and tell her that he would be home late after work. Leah overheard the conversation and said, "Honey, that means we have all day together."

At ten o'clock they made breakfast in the nude and ordered Chinese food for lunch. They spent the rest of the day making up for their lost weekend.

You see, when you read this book you might believe cheating is bad, but it isn't. In fact, there is nothing that you can say or do to convince these couples that what they're doing is wrong. They love their spouses and friends. They have seldom disrespected each other. The parties that were involved in this fun loving escapade really enjoyed it. Tony's last words were, "If cheating is wrong, I don't want to be right". Sandy figured that if her partner never found out, everything would be just dandy.

Both of the couples are still seeing other people and their partner still don't know. Sandy is pregnant with Tony's baby; and this time, she made damn sure Sean used a condom! Meanwhile, Sandy's friend, Kashia, tied the knot with Uriel. She is also expecting a baby. Sean got married and Tianna is pregnant with her first child. Sean and Sandy still go to their favorite place in New Jersey. The Princess Leah of France only loves one man and she's willing to share him because he does it good and she loves him.

Printed in the United States
by Baker & Taylor Publisher Services